ON CONSTITUTIONAL DISOBEDIENCE

INALIENABLE RIGHTS SERIES

. . .

Mark V. Tushnet
WILLIAM NELSON CROMWELL PROFESSOR OF
LAW
HARVARD LAW SCHOOL

J. Harvie Wilkinson
JUDGE
U.S. COURT OF APPEALS FOR THE FOURTH
CIRCUIT

GEOFFREY STONE AND OXFORD UNIVERSITY PRESS GRATEFULLY ACKNOWLEDGE THE INTEREST AND SUPPORT OF THE FOLLOWING ORGANIZATIONS IN THE INALIENABLE RIGHTS SERIES: THE AMERICAN LIBRARY ASSOCIATION THE CHICAGO HUMANITIES FESTIVAL THE AMERICAN BAR ASSOCIATION THE NATIONAL CONSTITUTION CENTER THE NATIONAL ARCHIVES

On Constitutional Disobedience

. . .

Louis Michael Seidman

OXFORD
UNIVERSITY PRESS

OXFORD
UNIVERSITY PRESS

Oxford University Press is a department of the University of Oxford.
It furthers the University's objective of excellence in research,
scholarship, and education by publishing worldwide.

Oxford   New York
Auckland   Cape Town   Dar es Salaam   Hong Kong   Karachi
Kuala Lumpur   Madrid   Melbourne   Mexico City   Nairobi
New Delhi   Shanghai   Taipei   Toronto

With offices in
Argentina   Austria   Brazil   Chile   Czech Republic   France   Greece
Guatemala   Hungary   Italy   Japan   Poland   Portugal   Singapore
South Korea   Switzerland   Thailand   Turkey   Ukraine   Vietnam

Oxford is a registered trademark of Oxford University Press
in the UK and certain other countries.

Published in the United States of America by Oxford University Press
198 Madison Avenue, New York, NY 10016

Library of Congress Cataloging-in-Publication Data
Seidman, Louis Michael.
On constitutional disobedience / Louis Michael Seidman.
p.   cm. — (Inalienable rights series)
Includes bibliographical references and index.
ISBN 978-0-19-989827-5 (hardback)
1. Constitutional law—United States—Philosophy.   2. Constitutional law—
United States—Interpretation and construction.   I. Title.
KF4550.S375 2013
342.73001—dc23   2012023032

1 3 5 7 9 8 6 4 2

Printed in the United States of America
on acid-free paper

For Judy Mazo

Contents

· · ·

CONTENTS

Editor's Note

. . .

We hold these truths to be self-evident, that all men are created equal, that they are endowed by their Creator with certain unalienable Rights....

—*The Declaration of Independence*

Several volumes in the *Inalienable Rights* series have offered competing approaches to the challenge of constitutional interpretation, including Larry Tribe's *The Invisible Constitution*, David Strauss's *The Living Constitution*, Goodwin Liu, Pamela Karlan, and Christopher Schroeder's *Keeping Faith with the Constitution*, and Jay Wilkinson's *Cosmic Constitutional Theory*. Other volumes, such as Richard Epstein's *Supreme Neglect*, Lee Bollinger's *Uninhibited, Robust, and Wide-Open*, Alan Dershowitz's *Is There a Right to Remain Silent*, and Martha Nussbaum's *From Disgust to Humanity*, attempt to give meaning to specific constitutional provisions. Indeed, every volume previously published in this series grapples in one way or the other with the vexing task of giving concrete meaning to the often vague and open-ended provisions of the American Constitution.

Mike Seidman's *On Constitutional Disobedience* asks a very different question: Why should we care at all what the Constitution says? Seidman pulls us back to square one and insists that we reclaim our democracy from the dead hand of the past. As he asks, "if we are convinced after taking everything into account that one course of action is right, why should we take another course of action just because of words written down on a piece of paper more than two hundred years ago?" "Who in their right mind would do this?"

After carefully reviewing all the arguments for why we *should* "do this," Seidman concluded that our national obsession with the binding effect of the Constitution has contributed to the "general perception that our political dialogue is seriously broken." This is so, he explains, because "when arguments are put in constitutional terms, they become absolutist and exclusionary." Such claims "have poisoned our political discourse," and to restore civility to our democracy "we must learn to express our disagreement in terms that do not invoke our nation's supposedly defining commitments." The word "supposedly" is critical to Seidman's critique.

Seidman acknowledges, of course, the goal of abandoning constitutional law will be difficult to achieve. Old habits die hard. But in *On Constitutional Disobedience*, Seidman poses deep, provocative and insightful questions about our conventional national wisdom. By so doing, he calls the entire enterprise of constitutional law into question.

Geoffrey R. Stone
June 2012

ON CONSTITUTIONAL DISOBEDIENCE

Introduction: The Gaudy Contradictions
of American Constitutionalism

WHEN THE 112TH Congress met for the first time on January 6, 2011, members of the House of Representatives made history by reciting aloud the Constitution of the United States. The unprecedented reading managed to combine high drama and low farce in approximately equal doses.

Some moments were authentically inspiring. The recitation began with newly elected Speaker John Boehner intoning the majestic words of the Constitution's preamble. Congressman John Lewis, a civil rights hero who almost a half century earlier stood his ground on the Edmund Pettus Bridge while rampaging police split his head open, read the powerful commands of the Thirteenth Amendment. Only two days before she was gunned down in Tucson, Congresswoman Gabrielle Giffords recited the First Amendment's guarantees of freedom of speech and religion.

But if the planners of the exercise thought that they could isolate this celebration of constitutional text from the often tawdry, frequently absurd, almost always hyper-partisan reality of contemporary American politics, they were sadly mistaken. It turned out, for example, that the leadership had decided against actually reading all of the constitutional text. Instead, they mandated recitation of a bowdlerized version so as to avoid forcing members to read aloud embarrassing parts of the document that, for example, endorsed slavery. Before the reading could get under way, there was a ludicrous and unseemly squabble on the floor about which parts of the document would be read and which parts politely ignored.

When the reading finally began, members at first paid close attention and followed along with their pocket Constitutions. As the recitation progressed through some of the Constitution's more obscure clauses, however, they seemingly lost interest. Members consulted their smartphones and fidgeted in their seats. Some left the chambers. When the reading reached Article II, sec. 1, providing that the president must be a "natural-born citizen," a woman in the gallery rose and shouted "Except Obama! Except Obama! Help us, Jesus! My name is Theresa." She was escorted out of the chambers before she could fully identify herself.

In short, the occasion was marked by an incongruous mixture of reverential invocation of constitutional text as a symbol of national unity, cynical disregard for and boredom with what the text actually said, and bare-knuckled efforts to utilize the text for contemporary political purposes. It perfectly captured the gaudy contradictions at the center of modern American constitutionalism.

In this book, I explore the too often ignored issue at the center of these contradictions. My topic is the problem of constitutional obedience. Should we, after all, feel obligated to obey this deeply flawed, eighteenth-century document? Suppose, for example, President Obama really were born outside the United States. Why should this matter to us?

If the organizers of the congressional reading thought about this question at all, they no doubt assumed that the answer was easy. I am certain that many of the readers of this book share this view. A proposal that we systematically ignore the Constitution will strike many as stupid, evil, dangerous, or all three. But the congressional reading itself demonstrated that the arguments for constitutional obedience are far more fragile than commonly acknowledged.

To see the problem, we need to start with the fact that the newly empowered House Republicans had a decidedly contemporary motive for their celebration of this ancient text. The Republicans, and especially their Tea Party supporters, believe that the Constitution strongly supports political objectives like defeating national health care, preserving gun rights, sharply restricting taxation, and limiting the power of the federal government. It was for just this reason that they coupled the opening ceremony with a change in House rules that made new legislation subject to a point of order if it was unaccompanied by a statement of the provisions of the Constitution that authorized it and an argument for its constitutionality. Precisely because the Constitution has near-sacred status, Republicans think that they can use it as a powerful political weapon to defeat their adversaries.

The question I want to address is whether we should accede to this power. Suppose, for the moment, that the Tea Partiers are right and that the Constitution means what they say it means. Why, then, should the rest of us obey its commands? For many of us, the Tea Party constitution is deeply pernicious. Put succinctly, it mandates a country that we do not want to live in. If forced to choose between obedience to such a document and fundamental principles of justice, shouldn't we choose justice?

Of course, the Tea Partiers may be misinterpreting the Constitution. Perhaps, as properly understood, the Constitution commands none of the results they favor. But if the document authorizes implementation of policies that Tea Partiers hate, then why should *they* obey its commands? Put more generally, why should *anyone,* on the Left, the Right, or in the center, renounce positions of policy and principle that she favors simply because those policies and principles are inconsistent with the Constitution?

The standard answer, of course, is that the Constitution, in the words of its preamble, was adopted by "We the People." The framers provided for state ratification by popularly chosen state conventions. For a time, debate over the selection of delegates to the conventions and over the proposed constitution itself consumed the country. The United States engaged in what amounted to a long-running national seminar on governance, political theory, and the kind of country its citizens wished to live in. The upshot was ratification by all thirteen states. Because "We the People" chose to be bound by this text, "We the People" are now obligated to obey it.

Unfortunately, there are many things wrong with this story. We can start with the awkward fact that the Constitution itself was born of disobedience. The delegates were summoned to Philadelphia to amend the existing Articles of Confederation, not to displace it. They immediately decided to ignore their mandate as well as the requirements spelled out in the Articles for its alteration. Why should we feel obligated to obey their handiwork when they themselves disobeyed the legal limits on their power?

Perhaps the voice of the people should be allowed to override the law, but at this late date, we cannot know what the people's voice actually said. As historians of ratification have demonstrated, the process was shot through with political shenanigans, systematic suppression of the views of the Constitution's opponents, misrepresentation, and outright coercion. We can only guess at what a majority of people who participated in the ratification process "really" thought. Indeed, it is a myth to suppose that the people can ever somehow speak clearly and directly without their voice being distorted by flawed, real-world political mechanisms that translate their voice into a legal mandate.

This problem is compounded by the fact that many people were not considered "people" in late eighteenth-century America. No women,

African Americans, or Indians and few individuals without property were allowed to cast votes. More significantly, no one alive today had anything to do with the ratification process. As Thomas Jefferson famously insisted, the world belongs to the living. It is hard to see how even a pristine process that perfectly captured the views of eighteenth-century America can bind the very different people who populate the United States today.

These are all reasons that ought to give us pause about the Constitution's binding force. But there is another reason that is at once simpler and more powerful than any of these. The test for constitutional obligation arises when one thinks that, all-things-considered, the right thing to do is X, but the Constitution tells us to do not-X. It is only in this situation that constitutional obligation really has bite. It is only then that if we obey the Constitution, we are doing so for the sole reason that we are bound to obey. But who in their right mind would do this? If we are convinced after taking everything into account that one course of action is right, why should we take another course of action just because of words written down on a piece of paper more than two hundred years ago?

As a practical matter, in the real world, almost no one changes her opinion about anything important just because of the Constitution. We regularly avoid this distasteful necessity by reading the Constitution so as to support the opinions we already hold. Progressives insist on their reading while conservatives insist on theirs. We are asked to believe that it is no more than coincidence that the supposedly good faith and politically neutral effort of both sides to understand the same eighteenth-century text leads each side to read it in a fashion that embodies its own contestable political programs while delegitimating the programs of its adversaries. Or, more precisely, we are asked by each side to believe that its disinterested reading leads to this result, while the other side's manipulation of text and history amounts to a cynical, politically motivated effort to distort the Constitution's true meaning.

There is a way to read the Constitution that avoids this sort of division. The Constitution could be a symbol of national unity if we focused on its commands at the most abstract level. Almost no one disagrees with the great goals of forming a more perfect union and providing for the common defense. Almost everyone supports liberty and equality in the abstract. We could all embrace the Constitution if we read it as a work of art, designed to evoke a mood or emotion, rather than as a legal document commanding specific outcomes.

I believe that this is, in fact, the way that the Constitution should be read. The Constitution might provide us with a common vocabulary we could use to discuss our disagreements. Speaking on the 150th anniversary of the Constitution's ratification, Franklin Roosevelt endorsed this version of constitutionalism:

> The Constitution of the United States was a layman's document, not a lawyer's contract. That cannot be stressed too often. Madison, most responsible for it, was not a lawyer; nor was Washington or Franklin, whose sense of the give-and-take of life had kept the Convention together.
>
> This great layman's document was a charter of general principles, completely different from the "whereases" and the "parties of the first part" and the fine print which lawyers put into leases and insurance policies and installment agreements.

The problem, though, is that this reading sidesteps rather than solves the problem of obedience. The obligation of obedience arises only when we are asked to do something that we otherwise would not want to do. But everyone can support their political agenda by referring to constitutional ideals at the most abstract level. If the Constitution allows all of us to do whatever we want to do, then the problem of obedience never arises. It makes sense to talk about obeying the law, but no sense to talk about obeying a symphony or a painting.

In the rough and tumble of contemporary politics, neither side is interested in inspiring us with a work of art that requires nothing. Both sides want to treat the Constitution as a law that commands real outcomes. The upshot is that both progressives and conservatives are content to beat each other around the head and shoulders with charges of constitutional infidelity.

In this book, I argue that this is no way to engage in serious and authentic dialogue about the issues that divide us. We should give up on the pernicious myth that we are bound in conscience to obey the commands of people who died several hundred years ago. Rather than insisting on tendentious interpretations of the Constitution designed to force the defeat of our adversaries, we ought to talk about the merits of their proposals and ours.

Could the country survive this sort of honest airing of our differences? Defenders of constitutionalism argue that the abandonment of constitutional obligation would lead to chaos or tyranny. Their worries take a variety of forms. Sometimes, the concern is about settling disputes concerning the nuts and bolts of government. Without a constitution, how would we decide how long a president should serve or, even, whether there should be a president? How would we know when a bill became a law or whether someone claiming to be a senator really was one?

Others argue that the Constitution has served us well for over two hundred years and that there is little reason to believe that better arrangements are on offer. In particular, the Constitution provides vital protections for civil liberties. Without it, nothing would stop the government from establishing an official religion, jailing dissidents, or seizing all private property.

Still others are willing to recognize that constitutionalism is a myth, but they claim that it is a necessary one. Even if it is empty or regularly disregarded, the Constitution serves as a symbol of national unity, a secular religion. Without it, we would lose the necessary illusion that we are one people with a common history and destiny.

There are good reasons to be skeptical about these arguments. Have powerful actors really abstained from violating civil liberties just because of words written on a piece of paper? Are people really incapable of coordinating their activities and avoiding chaos without a constitution? Does the success of our country really depend on belief in a myth?

I address these questions at length in the rest of this book. For now, it is enough to note a contradiction at the root of all of these positions. As we have already seen, constitutionalists celebrate our founding document because it is an act of popular sovereignty—a command of "We the People." Popular sovereignty, in turn, entails a faith that left to their own devices ordinary people can make decisions about their own lives and about the nature of their government. But insistence on constitutional obligation rejects just this faith. When a political actor tells someone "you must do this because the Constitution requires it," the actor demands that people forsake their own deeply held moral and prudential judgments and obey commands promulgated by others. In this sense, the case for constitutional obedience is self-refuting. In the name of self-governance, it insists that people should not be allowed to make unfettered decisions about the questions that matter most to them.

Perhaps the people cannot be trusted to make these decisions for themselves. But if that is true, we ought to stop pretending that we have a polity based on popular sovereignty. Paradoxically, if instead we are to remain faithful to the great goals of the Constitution, we must first free ourselves from the yoke of constitutional obligation. Constitutionalists need to stop making deeply authoritarian demands about what we must do. Once they stop, "We the People" can begin the kind of open-ended and unfettered dialogue that is the hallmark of a free society.

CHAPTER ONE

. . .

The Argument Briefly Stated

THE AMERICAN CONSTITUTION is the oldest currently in force in the world. It was written generations before the advent of the technological, material, cultural, and moral conditions that define modern American life. When the framers did their work, America was a small, preindustrial society huddled along the eastern seaboard. A large portion of the country's economy depended upon slave labor. Travel was arduous and treacherous. Communication beyond one's immediate environment took weeks or months. The framers knew nothing of nuclear weapons, mass production, multiculturalism, cell phones, professional sports, modern birth control, or global warming. They had never heard of Martin Luther King Jr., Bill Gates, Albert Einstein, Adolph Hitler, or Lady Gaga. It is impossible to imagine what they would have thought of women's liberation, evolution, gay marriage, psychoanalysis, reality television, globalization, or the war on terror.

This gap between them and us provides a powerful argument for giving up on constitutional obedience. The sheer oddity of making modern decisions based upon an old and archaic text ought to give constitutionalists pause. They insist that we follow the commands of people who knew nothing of our problems and have nothing to do with us, who are not even biologically related to most of us. In what sense are their hopes, fears, preoccupations, and obsessions our own?

Some defenders of constitutional obedience attempt to meet this objection by relying on the so-called "living Constitution." On this view, the Constitution can be brought up to date by reading its vague commands in light of contemporary realities. Yes, the framers would have been astounded to discover that, say, "due process of law" meant the right to engage in same-sex sodomy, but precisely because the framers did not understand our world, we should read their language in a modern context. On this view, the very decision to formulate constitutional commands in majestic generalities implies a decision to allow the language to change and grow over time.

Unfortunately, however, this response is vulnerable to a number of devastating objections. First, no one claims that all of the Constitution can be made "living." Some of its most pernicious provisions are as positively, absolutely dead as the Wicked Witch of the West. Unfortunately, though, unlike the Wicked Witch, dead constitutional language continues to rule from the grave.

For example, constitutional language creating the grotesquely malapportioned Senate, mandating a presidential election system that allows the loser of the popular vote to assume office, or providing no congressional representation for residents of the District of Columbia are hardly written in majestic generalities. As constitutional scholar Sanford Levinson has argued, provisions like these are "hard wired." Their specificity makes them resistant to reinterpretation, and they saddle us with results that few contemporary Americans would defend on their merits.

True, in theory, the language might be changed by constitutional amendment, but the amendment provisions of Article V are exceedingly cumbersome. These provisions are, themselves, hard wired. As a practical matter, they make the amendment process useless when powerful minorities benefit from the status quo.

What about more general guarantees like equal protection and due process of law? We can at least sometimes escape the tyranny of the past with regard to these provisions if we interpret them in light of contemporary realities. As many modern originalists complain, however, this freedom comes at the expense of authentic obligation. If "due process" means whatever contemporaries think that it ought to mean, then we are no longer bound by constitutional language in a meaningful sense. What originalists fail to point out, though, is that if we instead cabin the provisions by interpreting them according to their "original public meaning" or the framers' specific intent, we are stuck with eighteenth-century judgments about twenty-first-century problems.

Advocates of the "living Constitution" respond to this dilemma by insisting that the values expressed in these provisions are enduring even if the application of those values to facts on the ground changes over time. One might be forgiven, though, for suspecting that the values are enduring precisely because they do not bind us to very much. It does not require much work to construct an argument for or against almost any outcome based on "equality" or "liberty." For example, abortion rights protect the equality and liberty of pregnant women, but abortion prohibitions protect the equality and liberty of unborn children. To the degree that the results commanded by constitutional values are indeterminate, the obligation of constitutional obedience fails to take hold.

Suppose, though, that the values are at least occasionally determinate enough to decide contested cases. We still have not solved the fundamental riddle of obedience. Either contemporary Americans share these values or they do not. If we already share the values, then we will strive to implement them not because they are part of the Constitution, but because we agree with them. If we do not share them, then we remain without an answer to the question why we should be bound by a past generation's discredited moral intuitions.

Of course, contemporary Americans might be divided about particular values. Perhaps, for example, a majority of the people as a whole reach one conclusion about a value or about the application of a value, but a majority of the people in a particular state reach a different conclusion. Any society, including our own, must find a way to work out disagreements like this.

There are many possible methods. We might, for example, systematically promote compromise between conflicting value judgments. We might allow local communities to decide questions for themselves, or we might cede control to national majorities. We might even have an elite body like the Supreme Court make value judgments for all of us.

It is hard to imagine, though, that a sensible person would cede the value choice to a relatively small group of people who knew nothing about modern society, who are long dead, and who held values that virtually no American would accept today. Yet this is precisely what constitutional obedience demands.

This fundamental problem with constitutional obligation is not just theoretical. Insistence on constitutional obligation is a way that some people exercise power over other people. As free citizens, we have a right to be provided with a reason before such power is exercised. But people exercising the power of constitutionalism are usually excused from the obligation to provide reasons for why we should be bound by constitutional commitments. They need not respond to even the most powerful arguments premised on policy and principle for a course of action. Instead, they are empowered to say "no" just because of words written on very old parchment. Free Americans should not put up with this sort of arbitrariness and arrogance.

That, in a nutshell, is the argument against constitutional obedience. What are the arguments in favor? In what follows, I briefly summarize my best understanding of these arguments and explain, as an introductory matter, why they should not prevail. The first part of the chapter provides a thumbnail sketch of some of the major points constitutionalists regularly make along with brief responses. The second part outlines an answer to the theoretical claims made by constitutionalists. The third part begins the task of dispelling worries about the likely consequences of disobedience.

It is important to add that my ambitions for this chapter are very modest. I do no more than provide an introductory sketch of various arguments for and against constitutionalism. I hope to convince readers that there is a problem with constitutional obedience and that the simple responses to this problem do not resolve it. In the chapters that follow, I discuss in much more detail the harms produced by constitutionalism and the flaws in the arguments advanced by its defenders.

TEN ARGUMENTS FOR CONSTITUTIONAL OBEDIENCE
AND WHY THEY ALL FAIL

Suppose, then, that the Constitution, properly interpreted, commands us to do one thing, but that our all-things-considered judgment is that it is just, or wise, or prudent to do something else. Why should we privilege constitutional text over our all-things-considered judgment? Here are the main possibilities together with very brief rejoinders:

The Supremacy Clause of Article VI makes the Constitution the supreme law of the land

The Supremacy Clause states that "This Constitution, and the Laws of the United States which shall be made in Pursuance thereof; and all Treaties made, or which shall be made, under the Authority of the United States, shall be the supreme Law of the Land." This language clearly establishes that, *if we choose to obey the Constitution,* then it is the supreme law of the land. But the Clause has this effect only if the Clause, itself, is obeyed, and whether it, along with the rest of the

Constitution, should be obeyed is the very question in controversy. Obviously, no text can validate itself. If it could, then any of us could write our own constitution, declare it supreme, and thereby command the obedience of others. It follows that we must look outside the Constitution for reasons why we should follow its commands.

In Chief Justice John Marshall's words, "all those who have framed written constitutions contemplate them as forming the fundamental and paramount law of the nation."

Marshall is correct in his premise, but the conclusion that we should obey constitutional commands does not follow for reasons similar to those that defeat the first point. Of course, the framers of the Constitution wanted their commands to be obeyed. Why else would they have spent a hot, miserable summer behind closed doors and windows in Philadelphia? Anyone who asserts power wants their assertion to be successful. But the bare assertion of power coupled with a desire to succeed does not provide a reason for why we should obey. If it did, we would be obligated to follow the wishes of every petty tyrant who sought to inflict his will upon us.

"We the People" consented to the Constitution by duly ratifying it. We are therefore morally bound to obey it

Although constitutional apologists persist in ignoring or denying the fact, an important driving force behind the new Constitution came from speculators who had bought up Revolutionary War debt at pennies on the dollar and then wanted the national government to impose high taxes to ensure that the debt would be redeemed at face value. The Constitution was designed to reduce the power of the state governments that threatened these interests and, more broadly, to protect the emerging commercial class at the expense of farmers and debtors. The document was ultimately ratified, but not without considerable hanky-panky and coercion directed against opponents. Nothing like all the people participated in the Constitution's ratification. Large segments of the population, including women, slaves, American Indians, and people not owning property, were mostly excluded from the ratification process. Moreover, the process itself was arguably illegal. Amendments to the Articles of Confederation—the only thing that the Constitutional Convention was authorized to propose—required the unanimous consent of the states, whereas the Constitution provided for its own ratification when only nine of the thirteen states agreed. As if all this were not enough to dispose of this argument, the ratification process demonstrated at most that a majority of Americans then alive consented to be ruled by the Constitution. It does nothing to demonstrate that the people alive today consent. Why should we be morally bound by other people's mistaken judgments?

If we don't like the Constitution, we can always amend it

The amendment process spelled out in Article V of the Constitution is exceedingly cumbersome. Indeed, the American Constitution is more difficult to amend than any other national constitution in the world. As a practical matter, then, amendment is often not an effective alternative to disobedience. In any event, the amendment argument, like the Supremacy Clause argument, leads us in a circle. The very question in dispute is whether Article V, like the rest of the Constitution, should be obeyed. The answer to that question cannot rest simply on the existence of Article V.

The framers were wise men who wrote a document that provides a good framework for government

One might begin by questioning just how wise they were and just how good a framework they provided. Doubtless, the framers produced a document that marked an important advance in political theory. But the history of ideas did not end with their work. Today, many of their ideas seem strange, to say the least, and even when their judgments are not morally repulsive, many of them have been overtaken by events. Among other things, many of the framers believed that it was appropriate for some people to own other people, that a government need not concern itself with the views of non-whites, women, or people not owning property, and that a federal government with sharply constricted powers could effectively govern the nation. Even as amended and interpreted, the document they wrote has many anomalies, of which, perhaps, the most egregious is the overrepresentation of small states in the Senate.

Suppose, though, that we put all this to one side. Even if we stipulate the putative wisdom of the framers, the stipulation cannot provide a solution to our problem. Of course, *to the extent* that the judgment of the framers matches our own all-things-considered judgment—that is, *to the extent* that we think that they were wise—we should follow their commands. But then we are following constitutional commands not because we are obligated to do so, but because they coincide with our own all-things-considered judgment. Obligation takes hold only when there is a gap between a constitutional command, on the one hand, and our all-things-considered judgment, on the other. No matter how excellent the constitutional text, its excellence does nothing to explain the riddle of obedience when such a gap emerges.

If we did not obey the Constitution, the result would be anarchy or tyranny

One might start again by quarreling with the premise. Other successful, nonanarchic, and nontyrannical countries like the United Kingdom and New Zealand seem to do just fine without a written Constitution. In fact, as I discuss in chapter 3, *we* seem to have done just fine even though, in large ways and small, we have regularly violated a variety of constitutional provisions.

In any event, the tyranny and anarchy point can be assimilated into our all-things-considered judgment. Tyranny and anarchy are bad states of affairs. To the extent that following a constitutional provision wards them off, most people will reach an all-things-considered judgment that we should follow the provision. But we need to make contextual decisions about whether and when these risks are real and whether and when they outweigh countervailing reasons for ignoring the text. For example, Lincoln's refusal to obey constitutional text during the Civil War was arguably necessary to avoid tyranny and anarchy. So was Roosevelt's stretching of constitutional authority during the Great Depression. When the risks of unraveling are small, or (especially) when constitutional obedience itself might produce unraveling, the anarchy and tyranny argument does nothing to support constitutionalism. When the risks are large, constitutional obligation is unnecessary because almost everyone will make an all-things-considered judgment that we should follow constitutional text.

Without the Constitution, our civil liberties would be at risk

Once again, the examples of countries like the United Kingdom and New Zealand throw considerable doubt on this proposition. It is far from obvious that these countries, which lack written constitutions, have less robust traditions of protection for civil liberties than countries with constitutional protections. In our own country, Supreme Court enforcement of constitutional text has done little to protect civil liberties in moments of crisis when our commitment to them has been tested. For example, the Supreme Court did nothing to support the right of dissenters during World War I when many were thrown in jail or to protect the victims of McCarthyism when the anti-red scare was at its height. In any event, it is quite mysterious why anyone would think that words written on a piece of paper could possibly stand in the way of abusive exercise of government power. As many of the framers themselves recognized, the Constitution provides nothing more substantial than "parchment barriers." The only real protection for civil liberties is an engaged and tolerant public willing to respect and defend minority rights. For example, it is true that the Supreme Court declared racial segregation unconstitutional in 1954, but little real progress was made until almost a decade later when violent events in Birmingham and other parts of the south convinced northern whites that southern Jim Crow regimes were intolerable.

The framers were wise enough to write a constitution that is so vague that there is no need to disobey it

Much of the Constitution's language—for example, its guarantees of equal protection, due process, and the privileges and immunities of citizens—is open textured. Unfortunately, some of its most problematic provisions—for example, its requirement that the president be a "natural born citizen"—are not. To the extent that the language is open textured, its vagueness avoids but does not solve the problem of constitutional obedience. When the Constitution is so vague that we can always do whatever we want and still remain within its strictures, the problem of constitutional obedience never arises. In these situations, the document simply does not constrain us. When the Constitution is sufficiently precise to meaningfully constrain us, the problem of constitutional obedience arises but remains unsolved.

The method by which the Constitution was adopted guaranteed that the framers took the long view, which should be preferred to decisions made in the heat of a particular political moment

The premise is, once again, subject to challenge. On the one hand, the framers, like all politicians, were concerned with immediate political issues, and, as noted above, some of their motivations for writing the Constitution were quite unlovely. On the other, we should not underestimate the capacity of our contemporary leaders for statesmanship. Assuming for the sake of argument that the premise is correct, we still have to recognize that the framers' ignorance of future events makes their work both better and worse. There is a trade-off between the ability to abstract from short-term political considerations, on the one hand, and the inability to mold our rules to contemporary realities, on the other. Ultimately, we have no choice but to make our own, modern judgment about the extent to which the virtues of an abstract, long-range view outweigh the vices of following constitutional commands that are obsolete or fail to take account of current exigencies.

We should obey the Constitution because, based on our experience as a people, we have come to believe that it is good policy to obey

It is an important truth that the framers have no actual power to rule us from the grave. The Constitution has modern force only because we allow it to rule us. It is also undoubtedly true that many Americans accept the requirement of constitutional obedience as basic axiom of our system. But how many Americans have seriously thought about whether promoting a norm of constitutional obedience really is good policy? How many, instead, accept the axiom reflexively without considering its destructive effect on our political culture and on the goal of self-governance? The aim of this book is to generate serious thought on this subject. My hope and belief is that the norm of constitutional obedience cannot survive this sort of scrutiny. Of course, I may be wrong; readers may ultimately be unconvinced by my argument. But it is a mistake to cut off the argument before it begins with the circular assertion that the American people should obey the Constitution simply because the American people currently think that it is good policy to obey it.

WHAT CONSTITUTIONS ARE FOR, AND WHY WE
DO NOT NEED THEM

Can it really be that the arguments sketched above are all that the case for constitutional obedience amounts to? Surely, one might fairly suppose, there is more to the position than this? In fact, there is a little more, but not much. One can state these arguments at a higher level of abstraction and dress them up with the paraphernalia of fancy political theory, but, ultimately, we are just applying heavy doses of lipstick to the same old pig.

Still, on the assumption that sometimes high theory has value, this section moves back from specific arguments we have already discussed and addresses the problem from a more general perspective. From this vantage point, we can focus on the problem constitutions are supposed to address in the first place. I argue that the problem is real enough, but that constitutions do not solve it.

What follows is a ruthlessly stripped down version of the often-abstruse political theory said to support constitutional governance. The theory originates with the erosion of faith in the divine right of kings in the eighteenth century. If the will of God did not justify political authority, then what did? Of course, one possibility is that political authority is simply a fact in the world that has no justification. Perhaps it amounts to no more than power exercised by the strong against the weak. We may have prudential reasons for obeying our rulers—we do not want to be executed or imprisoned—but we have no moral reasons. An only slightly less bleak view holds that there is nothing that justifies the particular exercise of political authority, but that even tyrannical government is superior to the chaos that would result if there were no authority at all.

Classical liberal theorists were unsatisfied with either of these answers. They wanted a theory of government that gave people a reason in principle why government edicts should be obeyed. The problem of creating such a theory is especially acute in diverse societies where people have different religious commitments and different political and personal goals. In a political culture where everyone already agrees about most matters of importance, the problem of authority is much less serious. In modern societies where we not only tolerate but also prize a wide diversity of views, we need a theory for why political losers should accept their losses.

Liberal theorists solve the problem of political legitimacy by claiming that even people who disagree about political outcomes can agree on the method by which their disagreement can be settled. Such an agreement, once it is achieved, creates political legitimacy and prevents social disintegration. This meta-agreement—an agreement about what to do when we disagree—is enshrined in a constitution. It can take two forms. Sometimes, the meta-agreement commands assent because its terms are substantively just. One might believe, for example, that the constitutional guarantees of free speech and equal protection should be obeyed because they state important principles of political justice. Other constitutional provisions, say, the requirement that the president be at least thirty-five years of age or the precise division of authority between the federal government and the states, are not necessarily commanded by substantive justice. They nevertheless deserve obedience because of what we might call procedural justice. The key idea here is that it is better to accede to a particular method for settling our disagreements—even if it is imperfect—than to bicker endlessly about things that should be settled one way or the other.

To illustrate the force of this argument, consider the following parable: For years, a country has been wracked by a bitter and bloody civil war. Eventually, both sides agree to a written truce. The agreement is not perfect. It is a compromise. Still, it contains measures that are important to both sides. It is the best agreement that either side could reasonably expect to negotiate, and all agree that peace is better than endless war. Advocates for constitutional government argue that once the agreement is signed, both parties are obligated to obey its terms. There is no doubt that this argument has intuitive force, but will it really withstand analysis? In fact, the argument is riddled with problems.

The bare fact of the agreement provides no reason in principle why anyone should obey its terms. We have already seen that consent cannot bind future generations who were not at the table. It turns out, though, that it cannot even bind those who were at the table. After all, both sides reached the agreement under duress. The agreement reflects the balance of power between the parties at the time it is struck, and there is no guarantee that this balance is, itself, just. The parties "agreed" only because this was the sole means available to staunch the flow of blood. Of course, so long as the alternative to abiding by the agreement is continued or renewed civil war, both sides have a prudential reason to follow its terms. But if the balance of power shifts, or if the agreement proves too burdensome, there is no principled reason that a party should subordinate its conception of justice to a truce that was forced upon it. Liberated France had no obligation to respect the agreement that it had previously reached with Hitler. Nor should the Egyptian people feel bound to an agreement providing special protections for the military when those protections reflect no more than the military's power at the moment when they were granted.

Even if the unadorned fact of agreement does not produce an obligation to obey, there might be other reasons for obedience. Perhaps the terms of the original agreement are substantively just. But we have already seen that claims of substantive justice sidestep rather than support arguments for obedience. If the terms of the agreement are just, then they should be obeyed because they are just. The agreement itself adds nothing to this obligation.

Perhaps, then, the terms are procedurally just in the sense that they settle questions that are better resolved one way or the other than left open to continued dispute. Sometimes, no doubt, this argument has force. It would not be a good state of affairs if we had an argument about the length of a president's term every four years. But there is no reason to think that constitutional obligation is necessary to settle matters like this. The widespread sense that there is a need for closure provides motivation enough. In the United Kingdom, there is no written constitutional agreement that requires fresh parliamentary elections every five years, but the length of parliamentary sessions is nonetheless not a subject for debate.

Indeed, on some occasions, constitutional disobedience may do a better job of avoiding needless debate than constitutional obedience. As agreements age and become increasingly irrelevant to contemporary disputes, it may well be that departures from them, rather than mindless adherence to them, will best produce civic peace.

None of this is to deny that civic peace is a good. Liberal theorists were right to focus on how it can be maintained in a just fashion. The irony, though, is that the best strategy for a just peace involves forsaking, rather than insisting upon, constitutional obligation. An approach that focuses on obedience is bound to produce simmering grievances that, left unattended, risk political unraveling. Stubborn insistence that a society's foundational document embraces principles that some citizens find abhorrent is bound to lead to disaffection.

We might better achieve civic unity with a constitution that provides a vocabulary and an abstract set of ideals that everyone can agree to. Precisely because everyone can agree to them, these ideals command nothing. We have already seen that under this approach to constitutionalism, obedience plays no role. An obligation to obey takes hold only when one has a duty to do something one would otherwise not want to do. A poetic constitution does not compel anyone. The very indeterminacy of such a constitution might nonetheless entice people into a continued peaceful discussion about what is to be done. The realization that other people, who adhere to the same ideals we do, reach radically different conclusions about what those ideals entail might lead us to focus on the contingency and fragility of our own commitments. Even if we are unprepared to give up on those commitments, we might at least generate enough empathy for our opponents to want to resolve our differences peacefully.

At least that is the hope. Surely that hope is more consistent with our ideal of self-governance than the cynical effort to bludgeon people into accepting principles that they disagree with just because those principles are embodied in a document they had no role in creating.

THE CONSEQUENCES OF DISOBEDIENCE

The discussion in the previous section was on a high level of abstraction. But are there not real, practical problems that would be created by giving up on constitutional obedience? For example, how would elections be organized? How would we know the boundaries between federal and state power? How would the Supreme Court decide cases and justify its decisions?

In fact, the demise of constitutional obedience would produce less change than one might expect. As we have already seen, many provisions in the Constitution are extraordinarily vague and sweeping. These provisions already allow decision makers—whether Supreme Court justices, members of Congress, or ordinary citizens—to incorporate their contemporary all-things-considered judgments without bringing into question the binding force of text. Of course, there are other provisions that are much more specific. As I demonstrate in chapter 3, we have simply ignored some of these provisions when they have gotten in our way. We have done so without attracting much notice and without threatening the overall edifice of constitutionalism. If the collapse of a culture of obedience caused us to ignore other senseless provisions, so much the better.

It does not follow, though, that we would ignore all of the specifics. Our all-things-considered judgment will often be that the framers settled matters in more or less the right way. Even when we disagree with the framers, we will often conclude that it is better to have the matter settled one way or the other than to insist that it be settled the right way. We will therefore continue our current practices not because we are compelled to do so but because our all-things-considered judgment is that this is the best way to proceed.

There is a lurking difficulty with this scenario. In my argument so far, I have claimed somewhat simplistically that "we" would make all-things-considered judgments. But, of course, there is no disembodied "we." There are only political institutions—the state of Wyoming, the Food and Drug Administration, the president, and so forth—who claim the authority of "we." Without a constitution, how are "we" to express our decision to, say, have or not have a Supreme Court? How would "we" decide which institutions were authoritative?

This is a problem, all right, but it is not a problem that the Constitution can solve. After all, the framers have no actual power over us. Constitutional obedience ultimately rests on contemporary consent. But consent by whom and through what institutions? Constitutions cannot provide legally legitimate answers to these questions because every new constitution, itself, begins with an act that is illegal under the previous regime. For example, in 1787, there was no preexisting binding legal commitment to accept as law a document written by a convention in Philadelphia and ratified by nine of the thirteen states. On the contrary, the procedures used to ratify the Constitution were impermissible under the existing legal regime. Yet somehow the ratification process came to be seen as legitimate and late eighteenth-century Americans decided to respect the outcome of that process. In the same mysterious fashion, contemporary Americans can decide on the shape and power of their institutions.

For the reasons outlined above, it may well be true that contemporary Americans are satisfied with their existing institutions and the results those institutions produce. If so, upending a culture of constitutional obedience would have much less impact than is commonly supposed. If ending a norm of constitutional obedience has little practical effect, why bother? Although an end to constitutional obligation would not produce the results that many fear, it would have some salutary consequences. As we have already seen, in current political debate it is permissible, and sometimes highly effective, to counter an argument for a proposal with the assertion that "that's unconstitutional!" As things now stand, the only response to this assertion is "no it's not!" What follows, then, is a tendentious and ultimately beside-the-point argument about the meaning of the Constitution, with each side endorsing a reading of the text that just happens to support its political position.

If the culture of constitutional obedience were disrupted, these discussions would end, and, I think, our politics would be better for it. If nothing else, it is embarrassing to watch political participants on both the Left and Right twist constitutional language to meet their policy objectives. But the problem with modern constitutional argument goes beyond mere embarrassment. It is ultimately deeply authoritarian to try to end an argument by insisting on the sanctity of a particular text.

This move relieves the advocate of the duty we should all have—to explain and justify our positions to our fellow citizens. Free societies value authentic and open-ended dialogue about what is to be done. The claim that "it's unconstitutional" is a way to bring the discussion to an end. We would be much better off if we could agree to ban the claim from our political lexicon.

CHAPTER TWO

...

Obedience over Time

I HOPE THAT the previous chapter is sufficient to establish that constitutionalism faces serious problems. Given how serious those problems are, it is a wonder that constitutionalists are not more defensive. Why is it constitutional skeptics rather than constitutionalists who are feared, ridiculed, or, most often, simply ignored? Why is constitutional obligation assumed to be unquestionable common sense?

I cannot prove the point, but I believe that the very insecurity produced by the skeptical argument elicits the desire to marginalize it. The radical disconnect between us and the framers, far greater than the difference between, say, contemporary Americans and Mexicans, leads to subconscious or semiconscious anxieties about the legitimacy and the very possibility of political community. Just because the past is a stranger to us, we must invent lines of communication stretching over time. Without those lines of communication, we have no way to explain why we are Americans rather than Mexicans.

Most often, this anxiety does not take the form of an argument, but instead manifests itself in a desperate effort to change the subject. The first part of this chapter deals with this tactic.

Occasionally, though, the anxiety translates into something that actually looks like an argument for why we should be bound to the past. The argument takes a number of different forms. Sometimes, the claim is that our ability to precommit—to shield decisions from change over time—is itself an aspect of our freedom. Paradoxically, frustration of our current preferences vindicates our "true" preferences that were expressed at some earlier time. Sometimes, the claim is that judgments that emerged from particularly traumatic struggle, that were produced by an unusually engaged citizenry, or that were endorsed by supermajorities are entitled to special respect. A third version of the argument gets closest to what, I believe, actually motivates it. The claim here is that the myth of connection over time is essential to national identity. Just as Lincoln invoked "[t]he mystic chords of memory" when confronted with disunion, so we, too, must rely on our connection to a shared, if invented, past if we are to be an authentic community rather than merely a group of disconnected individuals who happen to inhabit the same territory.

It is tempting to dismiss these versions of the argument as what psychoanalysts call "reaction formation"—the attempt to defend against an anxiety by an obsessive and exaggerated rejection of the anxiety's source. But arguments advanced in good faith deserve a response on the merits, and so, in the second part of this chapter, I take this argument seriously and offer a variety of refutations. The chapter closes with an effort to deal with the underlying anxiety in what I hope is a more thoughtful and productive fashion.

TWO ARGUMENTS THAT MISS THE POINT

Before we discuss positions that attempt to engage the problem of constitutional obedience, we need to talk about all-too-common efforts to change the subject. As we have already seen, a key problem with constitutional obedience is that it misdirects political argument. Instead of talking about, say, whether national health care is good for the country, we end up talking about whether the framers would have thought that it was good for the country.

The problem of misdirection goes even deeper. It is not just that constitutional obedience misdirects political argument; the argument about constitutionalism itself has gone off track.

Typically, we talk about constitutional theory when presidents nominate Supreme Court justices or when the Supreme Court decides important cases. The debate has tended to focus on two questions: First, we have argued about the appropriate role of judges in a constitutional democracy. Is judicial invalidation of legislation inconsistent with democratic self-governance? Should judges be more deferential to political outcomes? Second, we have focused on the appropriate method of constitutional interpretation. Should judges be bound by the text of the Constitution? By the original intent of those who wrote the text? By the way the text was originally understood? Or should judges interpret the text in light of contemporary realities?

Each of these issues has generated endless debate both in the scholarly literature and in popular discourse. Many commentators have thought that the two problems are linked. On this view, the challenge is to come up with a theory of constitutional interpretation that justifies judicial power. For example, originalists, who think that the Constitution should be interpreted according to the "original public meaning" of its language or according to the framers' original intent, believe that only this interpretation can justify judicial decisions that frustrate democratic outcomes. In contrast, so-called process theorists have argued that judicial review can be justified insofar as it enables judges to ensure that political outcomes are consistent with what they view as the Constitution's theory of democracy. Still other theorists have insisted that judicial power is justifiable if judges interpret vague constitutional language in light of contemporary realities and what they see as the most attractive understanding of our prior legal decisions.

Each of these theories has some interest when considered on its own terms. In fact, though, none of them is worthy of the attention they have received. This is because all of them are obsessed with the false problems of judicial power and techniques of constitutional interpretation. They are simply ways of changing the subject so as to avoid the deeper issue we should really be addressing: Why should the members of any branch of government obey the Constitution in the first place?

Judicial Review

Very few Americans have ever heard of Alexander Bickel, a law professor who taught at the Yale Law School in the mid-twentieth century. Even fewer have read his most important book, *The Least Dangerous Branch*. Yet almost a half century after the book was published, Bickel's thesis continues to haunt constitutional debate. Unfortunately, though, Bickel made a crucial mistake—a mistake that we need to correct if we are ever to engage seriously with the real problems of constitutionalism.

Writing in the ponderous, portentous style favored then and now by legal academics, Bickel argued that judicial review was a "deviant institution." America was a democracy, but federal judges are not elected. They have lifetime appointments qualified only by the requirement that they exhibit "good behavior." They are deliberately shielded from political pressures, yet they regularly make decisions that settle political disputes. Why should they have the power to make public policy that binds the rest of us?

Bickel called this problem "the countermajoritarian difficulty." He did not go so far as to claim that it made judicial review altogether illegitimate, but he did argue that the difficulty was serious enough to mandate judicial deference and modesty. Although Bickel himself is rarely cited in public debate, his claim has been repeated countless times in newspaper editorials, talk show rants, pompous confirmation hearing speeches, and boring law school lectures.

In recent years, a growing body of scholarship has questioned just how countermajoritarian Supreme Court decisions really are. When one examines the history of the Court, it turns out that the justices have only rarely decided important cases in a fashion that frustrates popular majorities for very long. For the most part, the justices have been quite cautious. For example, the Court's defenders like to cite *Brown v. Board of Education*, the case where the Court held that segregated schools violated the Fourteenth Amendment, as an inspiring example of judicial solicitude for minority rights. In fact, *Brown* was supported by at least half the country on the day it was decided. Even so, the Court delayed serious enforcement of its decision for years until there were clear majorities supporting racial justice in the political branches. When those majorities collapsed, the Court's enforcement did as well.

Similarly, the tremendous political turmoil unleashed by its decision in *Roe v. Wade* upholding a woman's right to an abortion has tended to obscure the fact that a majority of Americans support at least a limited abortion right, albeit somewhat more limited than the right recognized by *Roe*. In some of the circumstances where majorities do not favor the right—for example, in cases of poor women who seek state-funded abortions, young women who want abortions without the consent of their parents, or women who need late-term abortion procedures—the Court has restricted the right.

On the few occasions when the Court has decided important cases in a fashion that frustrates political majorities, it has sometimes held sway for a while, but eventually, the political branches have gotten their way. For example, the pre–Civil War Supreme Court decided the *Dred Scott* case in a fashion that made the emerging Republican Party's insistence on limiting slavery essentially unconstitutional. The decision was quickly overtaken by events and, eventually, effectively overruled by the Reconstruction amendments.

Similarly, for a brief period the Supreme Court seemed on the verge of dismantling Franklin Roosevelt's New Deal. But after an epic struggle over Roosevelt's plan to change the Court's direction by "packing" it, the justices reversed course and, with the aid of numerous Roosevelt appointments, ended up validating all the New Deal measures that came before it.

In the middle of the last century, the Warren Court decided a series of criminal justice cases in a way that most Americans opposed. That opposition played a key role in Richard Nixon's victory in the 1968 election. Just as Roosevelt appointed justices who retreated from the Court's opposition to the New Deal, so too, Republican-appointed justices have overruled or sharply limited many Warren Court criminal justice precedents.

More recently, the Court has adjusted its position regarding issues like affirmative action, equal rights for women, gun control, and the death penalty in ways that align it with popular majorities. Of course, none of this means that the Court never decides cases in countermajoritarian fashion. Its decisions on matters like flag burning, school prayer, and campaign finance run counter to the views of popular majorities. The relationship between the Court and public opinion is complex. When the question before it is symbolic without much practical effect (flag burning), when the result is favored by intellectual elites (school prayer), or when the outcome benefits important economic interests (campaign finance), public opinion sometimes loses out. Still, the notion that the Court has generally stood against popular majorities is more fiction than fact.

The mechanism that causes judicial decisions to track public opinion is somewhat mysterious. In theory, the Court is shielded from political pressure. The justices do not have to stand for election. They serve life terms and their salaries cannot be reduced while in office. But in practice, they must depend on the political branches for enforcement of their decisions. Moreover, Congress and the president have a number of means at their disposal to discipline a Court that is too far out of step with prevailing political values. Congress controls the appropriations that fund the Court's operations. It can limit the Court's jurisdiction to hear cases. It can and has overruled unpopular decisions by constitutional amendment. In extreme cases, it can impeach a justice. These potential mechanisms are rarely or never used, but that may be because the justices realize they are available and therefore do not decide cases in a way that would trigger them.

To be sure, the justices do not often have to worry about political retaliation, but that is only because they are not predisposed in the first place to decide cases in a way that would trigger it. To get on the Supreme Court, a justice must be chosen by the president and confirmed by the Senate. This is a process exceedingly unlikely to produce someone who is anything but a cautious, politically conscious lawyer well within the political mainstream. There have been a few justices who do not fit this description. During the latter part of his time on the Court, William O. Douglas was an authentic radical and, perhaps, Clarence Thomas is one now. But the chances that justices who favored results radically different from prevailing political forces would achieve a working majority of the Court are virtually nil.

For all these reasons, both the fear and hope that the Court will serve as an important counterweight to popular majorities are overstated. In Harvard Law Professor Michael Klarman's apt phrase, the Court is "neither hero nor villain." It is neither the heroic defender of civil liberties nor the villainous protector of minority privilege that its supporters and detractors imagine it to be.

These observations are a significant corrective to Bickel's worry about the "countermajoritarian difficulty." For our purposes, however, they are not the most significant flaw in Bickel's argument. Suppose there were a countermajoritarian difficulty. Suppose that the Court in the name of the Constitution regularly decided important cases in ways that ran counter to popular opinion. Even if this were so, it would not reflect a problem with judicial review. Instead, it is a problem with constitutionalism itself. The key point that Bickel missed was that judicial review is merely a technique for enforcing the commands of the Constitution. The *Constitution* is countermajoritarian, at least in a certain sense. If we obey its commands, then we substitute eighteenth-century decisions for decisions made by contemporary majorities. But this countermajoritarian problem would exist whether or not judges were the enforcement method we relied upon. After all, if judges did not enforce the Constitution, and if we in fact prized constitutional obedience, then its commands would have to be enforced by someone else. So long as constitutional commands are taken seriously, that enforcer would have to act against the will of popular majorities.

Suppose, for example, that judicial review were abolished. We can imagine one of two possible outcomes. Perhaps legislators would then simply ignore the Constitution and pass whatever laws they liked. If this were the outcome, then the countermajoritarian difficulty would be solved, but the solution would come at the expense of constitutional obedience. The other possibility is that legislators themselves would take their constitutional obligations seriously. But if this were the outcome, it would mean that legislators would act on the basis of constitutional commands rather than on the basis of the wishes of their constituents. They would, in other words, be acting in a countermajoritarian fashion. True, their constituents would retain the power to punish them for these acts of defiance. Perhaps, if they were punished often enough, they would eventually either accede to popular will or be replaced with others who took their constitutional obligations less seriously. But then we would have once again given up on constitutional obedience.

The real countermajoritarian difficulty, then, is not with judicial power, but with the power we have ceded to the Constitution itself. The question Bickel ought to have addressed was whether that power is justified. Bickel and his many followers thought that judicial review was problematic because it was in tension with democracy. But once one sees that judicial review is only a technique for ensuring constitutional obedience, then Bickel's worry should extend to constitutional obligation.

As we have already seen, the extent to which the Supreme Court has acted in a countermajoritarian fashion has been greatly exaggerated. That fact, too, raises problems for believers in constitutional obedience. If judicial review is the primary method by which the Constitution is enforced, and if the Court regularly acquiesces to popular opinion, then we have to confront the question whether the Constitution is being enforced at all. If it remains mostly unenforced, then constitutional obedience cannot play the central role in our political culture that constitutionalists imagine it to play. Of course, it is possible that popular opinion itself aligns with the requirements of the Constitution. Perhaps the American people do not favor policies in the first place that the Constitution takes off the table. Remember, though, that constitutional obedience takes hold only when it leads people to do things that they would not otherwise do. We have to imagine, then, large majorities of Americans who would like to see things done, but revise their judgment and oppose doing them just because the Constitution prohibits these actions. Perhaps there are such people, but there is surely reason to be skeptical that there are many of them.

In subsequent chapters, I will return to the problem of measuring the extent of constitutional obedience. First, though, we must turn to a second obsession that drives current debate about constitutionalism.

Methods of Interpretation

While Bickel was developing his constitutional theories at Yale, his brilliant junior colleague, Robert Bork, was criticizing conventional learning about antitrust law. Bork eventually became interested in constitutional problems as well, and he and Bickel cotaught a seminar in constitutional theory. Ultimately, of course, Bork became much more prominent than his mentor. His failed nomination to the United States Supreme Court marks the beginning of the modern dispute about constitutional interpretation.

Bork famously argued that the countermajoritarian difficulty could be solved by a particular method of interpretation. He claimed that in a constitutional democracy, most questions should be left to the will of popular majorities. But importantly, not all questions. Americans believe in democracy, but they also believe in individual rights. The problem, then, is drawing a boundary line between majority power and individual (usually minority) rights. Bork pointed out that the problem could not be solved by leaving the task to either majorities or minorities. Giving majorities or minorities power to decide the scope of majority or minority power effectively prejudges the question. The only way out of the dilemma, Bork thought, was to assume majority power except in areas delineated by constitutional text, where individual rights were supreme. It followed that judges acted illegitimately unless they could tie their decisions to the original meaning of constitutional text.

Bork's contribution to constitutional debate was not much noticed outside the academy until President Reagan nominated him to the Supreme Court. Then, a firestorm broke, and the result was what amounted to an unusual public symposium on constitutional theory. Other scholars ridiculed Bork's version of originalism and pointed out the absurd and disturbing results it would yield if taken seriously. They advanced different methods of interpretation that focused more on the open texture of constitutional language. Bork's supporters responded with a vigorous defense of his approach.

Ultimately, Bork's nomination failed, but his theory nonetheless retains a powerful, if ambiguous, hold on the American imagination. On the one hand, politicians and judicial nominees continue to worship at the altar of originalism, perhaps on Henry IV's theory that Paris is worth a mass. Public attitudes toward originalism are more ambiguous. It is foolish to suppose that the public at large has anything like a considered view about the intricacies of constitutional theory. Still, if one talks about reflexive instincts rather than considered views, the popular impulse toward originalism continues to play an important role. On the other hand, Supreme Court justices on the Left and the Right regularly decide cases that cannot be justified by originalist methodology, and virtually no one can stomach the actual outcomes that a thoroughgoing commitment to originalism would produce.

Two remarkable facts stand out about this debate. First, despite the debate's intensity, virtually no one seems to disagree with Bork's core insight. People disagree about how the Constitution should be interpreted, but everyone seems to agree that the line between majority power and minority rights should be determined by the Constitution. Second, no one has bothered to offer a serious defense of this extraordinary proposition.

In Bork's original article, he claimed that any other solution left judges with the power to decide cases based on their uncontrolled discretion. But this claim is patently false. Judges who adopt nontextual theories of judicial review are not unconstrained. They are simply constrained by a theory or text different from the theory or text that constrains originalists. For example, judges who are guided by moral philosophy, by American traditions, by prior precedent, or by a commitment to democratic politics are not deciding cases according to whim. Perhaps more fancifully, judges who did not obey the Constitution might instead be constrained by the teachings of the Bible, John Stuart Mill, John Rawls, or the United Nations Declaration of Human Rights. Thus, the real issue is not constraint, but the choice of which theory or text will do the constraining. To be convincing, Bork must explain to us why the views of James Madison are more worthy of respect than the views of a host of other great thinkers.

Bork's answer was that popular majorities today want judges to follow the Constitution. In fact, as I have already noted, the public's complex, contradictory, and uninformed reaction to originalism makes this premise somewhat doubtful. The very fact that Bork's own nomination ultimately failed suggests that popular support for his view of constitutional obligation is less strong than he supposes. But even if his premise is correct, Bork himself provides a refutation of his own conclusion. As he himself claimed, we should not accede to popular majorities on issues of minority rights because to do so stacks the deck against minorities. It is quite mysterious how Bork can hold this view and yet also claim that majority support justifies obedience to the line between majority power and minority rights contained in the Constitution.

It follows from all this that Bork's approach as well as the various approaches of all of his critics beg rather than answer the question we need to address. *If* the Constitution were the appropriate source for our decisions bounding the domains of powers and rights, then we would indeed confront the problem of how to interpret it. But before we reach this point, we need to figure out *whether* the Constitution is the appropriate source. The sections that follow discuss the ultimately failed effort to explain why it is.

ULYSSES TROUBLES

Consider first the argument premised on precommitment. At its core, the enterprise of constitution writing amounts to an effort to control the future. That is how our own Constitution's framers saw their work. They meant the document they produced to be enduring and to shape the country over time. From our perspective, their work sometimes seems like a yoke that we press against when we try to pursue our own projects and goals. But for them, constitutional creation was an act of liberation and self-definition. As Chief Justice John Marshall wrote, "That the people have an original right to establish, for their future government, such principles as, in their opinion, shall most conduce to their own happiness is the basis on which the whole American fabric has been erected."

How can we possibly reconcile the images of a Constitution at once liberating and constraining? One possibility, of course, is that the Constitution was liberating for its authors precisely because it is constraining on us. On this view, constitutional obligation amounts to an intergenerational power grab that modern Americans should resist.

Constitutionalists want to avoid this conclusion, so they attempt to characterize earlier generations as our allies rather than our enemies. They want to demonstrate that our constitution not only liberated the framers, but liberates us as well. The most sophisticated efforts along these lines come from political theorists like Jon Elster and Thomas Schelling, who have claimed that precommitment can be an aspect of freedom.

Elster draws his central metaphor from Homer. Ulysses, curious about the beautiful and seductive song of the sirens, instructs his crew to plug their ears with beeswax and to tie him to the mast so that he can listen to the sirens without succumbing. Schelling relies on a different nautical analogy. In *Moby Dick,* Captain Ahab is attacked by the great white whale while at sea, and it is imperative that the crew cauterize the wound. In the absence of anesthesia, Ahab has himself tied down and instructs the crew to continue the procedure even if, in his agony, he tells them to stop.

Both examples illustrate how what may appear to be a limitation on freedom is actually an example of autonomy. Ulysses is able to achieve what he really wants—to listen to the sirens without succumbing— only by preventing himself from giving in to their enticements. So, too, Ahab understands that his true desire—to have the wound cauterized— can be achieved only by disabling himself from making choices that he will later regret.

The analogy to constitutionalism is obvious. As legal scholar Vincent Blasi has written, many constitutional provisions—Blasi focuses on free speech guarantees—are designed to prevent us from acting foolishly while in the grip of predictable pathologies. We know, for example, that when caught up in an immediate crisis, we may pay too little attention to civil liberties. So, during periods of calm, we precommit ourselves in ways that make it harder to give in to the sirens of oppression and that vindicate our "true" preferences.

There are two ways to confront this argument. One way is to attack the analogy. The analogy treats individual precommitment like the decisions made by Ulysses and Ahab as the same thing as societal precommitment. It therefore depends on the assumption that the people who precommit—the framers of constitutional provisions—are the same people who are later constrained by the precommitment. If they are not, then enforcement of the precommitment amounts to the assertion of power by one group over another rather than an exercise of freedom. After all, no one would claim that Ulysses acted freely if his crew tied him to the mast over his objections.

It follows that the precommitment argument rests on the possibility of a single, collective, national identity over time—a possibility that I address at the conclusion of this chapter. Suppose, though, that at least for the moment we concede this possibility. A second way to confront the argument is to problematize the freedom-enhancing claims for precommitment even in the case of a single individual. I pursue this line of criticism here.

In order to understand the problems with the argument, we need to tease out the various ways in which precommitment might be said to promote freedom. We can begin with a subtle distinction between the Ulysses and Ahab stories that, to my knowledge, no commentator has focused on. Ahab, like Ulysses, precommits so as not to give in to temptation, but Ahab, unlike Ulysses, would rather not undergo the temptation in the first place. Ahab is not a masochist. His first choice would be a painless operation. He chooses to precommit only because anesthesia is unavailable. In contrast, Ulysses had an analogue to anesthesia readily available. He could have sailed past the sirens without being tempted by their song if he had simply plugged his own ears as well as the ears of his crew. He does not do this because he actually wants to hear the siren song. For him, precommitment allows him to flirt with temptation with the assurance that he will not give in to it.

Other forms of freedom-enhancing precommitment fit neither the Ulysses nor the Ahab model. Often, precommitment arises in bargaining situations. One version protects against what economists call "opportunism." Suppose, for example, that I would like to hire you to paint my house. You might reasonably fear that after you finish the job, I will refuse to pay. That fear, in turn, might cause you not to enter the contract in the first place. If I can credibly precommit to pay if you do the job satisfactorily, we can reach an agreement that benefits both of us.

Precommitment as an adjunct to this sort of bargaining seems benign. It creates value for both parties. Still another form of precommitment serves as a means by which one party can best the other. Many people are familiar with the game of "chicken" as played in the classic movie "Rebel without a Cause." In the game's standard form (actually not the form played in the movie), two cars head towards each other at full speed; the driver who does not swerve wins. If I can precommit not to swerve by, say, disabling the steering wheel and if I can credibly communicate the precommitment to the other driver, I am certain to win. Here, my ability to bind myself to otherwise irrational action means that the other party has nothing to gain and everything to lose by hanging tough.

Another famous movie illustrates how the precommitment might work. In "Dr. Strangelove," the United States creates a "doomsday machine" designed to launch retaliatory missiles automatically if the Soviets attack. The theory behind the doomsday machine is that by credibly communicating a precommitment to mass destruction that might otherwise seem irrational, the United States can successfully deter its enemy. There are real-world examples of this strategy as well. For example, after his presidency ended, Richard Nixon claimed that he had deliberately created the impression that he was capable of irrational action as a method of increasing his bargaining power with foreign governments.

How do these various models of precommitment map onto constitutional precommitment? The most straightforward application grows out of Ahab-like precommitment. As we have already seen, constitutional theorists defend obedience on the ground that decisions made at an earlier time reflect our true preferences. Restrictions on what we want to do now are, therefore, paradoxical manifestations of freedom.

Arguments for Ulysses-like precommitment are less common in the literature, but they, too, have some force. On this view, constitutional limits are actually enabling because they permit government officials to do things that we might worry about without a precommitment. Precommitment permits us to secure benefits by going right up to a line that ought not be crossed. Consider, for example, the Fourth Amendment prohibition against unreasonable searches and seizures. We do not want to live in a police state, but we do want effective law enforcement. Without a precommitment drawing a sharp line, we might well be worried that police would gradually succumb to the siren call of overly aggressive invasions of individual liberty. Ironically, precommitting to a set of clear limitations allows us to secure the benefit of vigorous policing that we might be afraid to permit if we lacked assurance that the police would go no further.

What about precommitments to guard against opportunism? The provisions protecting private property and prohibiting the impairment of contracts in the Constitution are familiar examples of rules designed to serve these ends. They allow people to plan and make investments without worrying that the government will later seize the wealth produced by those investments. And on a higher level of generality, the Constitution's promise of stable and limited government gives people some assurance that the context in which they plan their lives will not be radically altered.

Finally, "chicken"-like precommitments also play a role in constitutional law and history. It was just such a precommitment that permitted ratification of the Constitution in the first place. To simplify a very complicated story, at the time of ratification, there was widespread dissatisfaction with the Articles of Confederation but also widespread opposition to the proposed Constitution. Many Americans, perhaps a majority, favored ratification only if accompanied by the acceptance of various amendments. Others thought that there should be a new constitutional convention that would be empowered to change the draft. The Constitution's supporters cleverly structured the decision so that the ratifying conventions could choose only between unconditional ratification of the Constitution, on the one hand, and outright rejection of it, on the other. By successfully precommitting to a default position that most people thought unacceptable (return to the Articles of Confederation), they forced acceptance of the unmodified draft.

There are also provisions within the Constitution that can be understood as employing a "chicken" strategy. For example, Article II provides that if no presidential candidate receives a majority of the electors' votes, the choice of president is taken out of their hands and turned over to the House of Representatives. This default might cause electors to soften their positions and come to majority agreement. Similarly, the president is given the choice of either vetoing an entire bill, signing the measure, or allowing it to go into effect without his signature. The failure to provide for a partial or line-item veto means that Congress can play chicken with the president by conditioning approval of measures he desperately wants on his agreeing to measures that he strongly opposes.

What are we to make of these various forms of precommitment as exercises of freedom? We can start by dismissing the "chicken" strategy. As both "Rebel without a Cause" and "Dr. Strangelove" demonstrate, chicken is a very dangerous game. If both parties end up precommitting or if one side's precommitment is not effectively communicated, the result is disaster. More to our immediate point, though, whatever else might be said for it, the chicken strategy cannot be defended on autonomy grounds. True, if the strategy works, it gives one party the freedom to get her way, but only at the expense of the other party, who is forced to accept a result that she finds repugnant. In these cases, the freedom game is zero-sum. Worse, permitting chicken games gives the most power to the people who are the most irresponsible. The party least bothered by the risk of a disastrous head-on collision is the one who can most credibly threaten it.

It follows, I think, that the chicken game played by the Constitution's defenders at the time of the framing provides an argument against, rather than for, the Constitution's legitimacy. It turns out that even at the moment of the framing, the Constitution's precommitments were in some sense not freely undertaken. Moreover, in a modern setting, the entire argument for constitutional obedience can be conceptualized as an analogous giant chicken game. Like the Constitution's eighteenth-century defenders, modern constitutionalists want to confront us with a stark choice: Either we accept wholesale enforcement of the Constitution, complete with all of its silly or pernicious provisions, or we will have a head-on collision in the form of a war of all against all, chaos, and an end to our civil liberties.

Surely, we should think twice before giving in to this sort of bullying. Of course, it is sometimes just the case that failure to accept an unpalatable alternative leads to another outcome that is more unpalatable still. When this is so, there is no sensible choice but to swallow one's anger and give in. Before we do so, though, we do want to be certain that we have been presented with all the available alternatives. In the chapters that follow, I argue that the choice between constitutionalism and disaster is a false one. There is simply no good reason for why we cannot continue to abide by constitutional provisions that now seem sensible to us while jettisoning those that do not. For now, though, it is enough to see that pre-commitment as an adjunct to chicken games is a way for some people to exercise power over others, not a method for maximizing freedom.

Other forms of precommitment do not suffer from this problem. They present themselves as positive-sum games that maximize freedom by allowing us to accomplish goals we could not accomplish without tying our hands in advance. The main difficulty with each of these strategies is that the benefits of precommitment do not come for free. We pay in the coin of limitations on our present freedom, and it is not obvious that the benefit is worth the price.

Consider, first, precommitment to avoid opportunism. Suppose that at Time 1, A promises B that he will pay a certain amount if B paints his house. At Time 2, in reliance on the promise, B paints the house. At Time 3, A discovers that he is seriously ill and needs the money he had put aside to pay B to fund his medical care. Should he keep his promise?

A natural reaction to this dilemma is to point to the rights of B. It is unfair to him for A to get the benefit of a painted house without paying for it. This point is right, but it demonstrates only that A might have good reasons at Time 3 to pay B. When A makes the decision at Time 3, he will have to balance a number of considerations, and there is no reason that one of them should not be considerations grounded in B's rights or in A's moral obligation to B. Perhaps, too, with hard enough thought, A can figure out a way to get the medicine and to pay B.

The precommitment argument is different. Instead of providing reasons why A should pay B at Time 3, it presupposes that there is a conflict between what A wants at the two time periods. Suppose, then, that A has taken into account all of the arguments in favor of paying B and still concludes that the best thing to do is to use the money for medical treatment. Advocates of precommitment say that A should nonetheless pay B because his preference at Time 1 should take precedence over his preference at Time 3.

There are two difficulties with this position. First, it is conceptually difficult to imagine how such a precommitment could work when the precommitment is between different generations. When we are talking about A and B, both parties are currently alive and can use legal processes to coerce each other. But when we are talking about present and past societies, there is no analogous means of enforcement. Ulysses can direct his men to tie him to the mast at Time 1 and the ropes will hold at Time 2. The framers, however, have no actual power over us. The constitutional struggle is between factions and institutions that are here now. Of course, some of these factions and institutions may try to justify their positions by invoking past commitments, but if we accede to their wishes, that is ultimately because they have persuaded us or because they possess instruments of coercion, not because the framers have real power over us.

This leads to the second difficulty. If we are to evaluate the claims of present people who invoke prior commitments, we need to figure out why past preferences are more worthy of respect than current preferences. In the opportunism case, the argument for precommitment at first seems quite straight forward. What A does in this case will affect incentives in future cases. If A breaks his promise to pay B, future Bs will not agree to paint his house and, in the long run, A will be worse off.

Is the argument persuasive? It is of course correct that what A does now will affect future Bs, but it does not follow that enforcing the precommitment makes A better off. If the precommitment is enforced, A cannot buy the medicine, and there is no a priori reason to believe that the cost in the form of future distrust outweighs the benefit of securing the medicine. After all, when A makes the decision at Time 3, he knows that a decision to buy the medicine will destroy his reputation for promise-keeping and so prevent him from inducing future reliance. If he nonetheless decides that securing the medicine is more important than preserving his reputation, how can we be sure that this decision does not reflect his "true" preference?

A similar point can be made about Ulysses and Ahab precommitments. Ulysses ties himself to the mast because he does not want to give in to the temptation of the sirens. But suppose that when he hears their song, it is more beautiful than he ever imagined and he really does want to give in. Is it so obvious that his preference before he had experienced the temptation is more authentic than his preference while he is experiencing it?

Similarly, suppose that Ahab instructs the surgeon to go ahead with the procedure even in the teeth of his order to stop it. Suppose, further, that once the procedure begins, the pain is worse than Ahab could have possibly imagined. If Ahab now orders the surgeon to stop, why should we suppose that this order is less a manifestation of his "true" preferences than his earlier order to keep going?

In each of these cases, the argument for precommitment is incomplete because it does not include a defense for the proposition that decisions in some settings are systematically more worthy of respect than decisions in other settings. If there is authentic conflict between what an actor wants at two different times, we need an account for why an earlier decision is wiser, or more just, or better reflects the actor's actual preferences than a later decision.

Perhaps there is such an account in the Ulysses and Ahab situations, although I must say that I am uncertain what it would look like. Even if there is, though, it does not follow that such an account is possible in a constitutional setting. As we have already seen, the problem in this setting is more acute because our Constitution is old and written against a very different social background. Both Ulysses and Ahab knew something about what the future held, but the framers of the American Constitution understood very little about modern America. Why are their uninformed preferences better than our informed ones?

A fair amount of modern constitutional theory is designed to fill in this gap, and those efforts are the subject of the next section.

SUPERMAJORITIES AND "CONSTITUTIONAL MOMENTS"

One argument for respecting past constitutional decisions rests on the special hurdles that have to be overcome in order to entrench those decisions. In the United States, the original Constitution took effect only after it was approved by popularly elected ratification conventions in nine of the thirteen states. New constitutional provisions can be added only if approved by an extraordinarily cumbersome amendment process.

In an important article, constitutional scholars John McGinnis and Michael Rappaport argue that these supermajority requirements provide built-in protection against unwise entrenchments. Their argument is complex and technical, but the driving intuition is clear enough: Measures that survive this extraordinary process are likely to reflect societal consensus, to be the product of deep deliberation, and to be free of narrow partisanship. It is therefore a mistake to disregard these measures merely because a contemporary majority disapproves of them.

No doubt, McGinnis and Rappaport have a point, but they also underestimate the pathologies that supermajority requirements build into the system. For example, and paradoxically, supermajority requirements empower small minorities. The ability of such minorities to block the adoption of constitutional provisions gives them the opportunity to hold even large majorities hostage. The result may be the entrenchment in the Constitution of special interest measures opposed by the majority of citizens. Some of the most egregious provisions in our own Constitution—for example protecting slavery or establishing the composition of the Senate—probably fit within this category. McGinnis and Rappaport do not explain why provisions that entrench special-interest compromises are worthy of our respect hundreds of years later.

Constitutional provisions may also exhibit a related pathology. When it proves impossible to assemble a supermajority to support a measure, constitution writers often settle on vague, bridging language that everyone can claim supports their position. Our Constitution is full of language of this sort. For example, the sweeping language of the privileges and immunities and equal protection clauses of the Fourteenth Amendment was broad enough to paper over disagreements

about what, precisely, should be prohibited. It is unclear how later inter-
preters should react to such language. If they ignore the guarantee entirely, they are giving up on constitutional obligation. But if they
interpret it so as to favor one side or the other of the historical debate,
they invent a resolution of the conflict that the framers themselves
could not—and did not—resolve.

McGinnis and Rappaport claim that the fact that constitution
makers operate under a partial "veil of ignorance" means that their work
is entitled to special respect. Because constitutions are entrenched
against change, the drafters cannot know whether their allies or enemies will benefit from constitutional language in future controversies.
Following John Rawls, McGinnis and Rappaport claim that this uncertainty pushes toward fairness and against partisan exercises of power in
the drafting process.

But the veil of ignorance can also introduce another sort of pathology. Suppose it is true that rules enacted by supermajorities have all the
virtues that McGinnis and Rappaport claim for them. This means that
the rules are likely to produce good results for the society that existed at
the time they were written. But precisely because constitutional framers
cannot know how the language they write will intersect with a future
world, there is no guarantee that their rules will produce good results
for future societies. Consider, for example, the division of war-making
authority between the executive and legislature. The framers were able
to assemble a supermajority for a system under which only Congress
could declare war. Suppose we stipulate that that system made sense in
a world where armies fought on horseback and with muskets and it
took ships months to cross the Atlantic. There is no reason to believe
that it will also make sense in a world of nuclear weapons and intercon-
tinental ballistic missiles.

A final problem: McGinnis and Rappaport ignore the fact that entrenching action against ordinary majorities actually involves two decisions rather than only one. They focus on a decision on the merits of a

proposed measure and claim that decisions reached by supermajorities will be better on that score. But, apart from the merits themselves, there is a separate issue about whether future generations should be permitted to reach a different conclusion about the merits. After all, no one claims that all decisions—even all wise decisions—should be entrenched against future majorities. What sorts of policies should be entrenched? There is no guarantee that drafters of constitutions will answer this second question wisely. The risk is that temporary supermajorities will use their power to entrench measures not because the measures embody the sort of policies that should be shielded from majority control, but simply because they have the power to do so.

We do not have to speculate about this danger. Consider, for example, the Eighteenth Amendment, which prohibited the "manufacture, sale, or transportation of intoxicating liquors" in the United States. In 1919, the year of ratification, a supermajority could be mustered in support of the measure. Yet almost no one today thinks that this sort of provision should be entrenched against future shifts in public opinion.

Fortunately, it proved possible to assemble a new supermajority to undo the Prohibition experiment, but there is no reason to suppose that we will always be so lucky. In fact, the Constitution contains scores of mundane rules that cannot be changed by popular majorities. To take two more or less random examples, the Constitution provides that no one can become a senator until she reaches the age of thirty, and that when a veto override is voted upon, the names of all persons voting for and against the override shall be entered into the journal of each House. These rules are not as disastrous as Prohibition; perhaps they are sensible. Still, it is hard to see why these rules and many others like them should be immune from majoritarian revision.

For all these reasons, the supermajority requirement standing alone is insufficient to explain why we should prefer past decisions to present ones. Perhaps, though, that requirement taken together with special circumstances surrounding the past decision will do the trick.

On the eve of the Civil War, abolitionists were a tiny minority. Indeed, as Lincoln assumed office, Congress enacted and Lincoln endorsed a constitutional amendment that would have permanently protected slavery from federal interference. Ironically, had it been approved by the states, it would have become the Thirteenth Amendment.

But then the war came. Hundreds of thousands were killed, among them black volunteer troops who fought gallantly for the Union cause.

This searing experience had a dramatic effect on northern public opinion. It became essential to give some meaning to the slaughter. As Lincoln famously claimed, the war became a struggle to produce "a new birth of freedom." And, so, when the war ended, the Reconstruction Congress dramatically reworked the Constitution, writing into it the actual Thirteenth Amendment, prohibiting slavery, as well as the Fourteenth and Fifteenth Amendments, providing permanent guarantees of equality, liberty, and political freedom.

These decisions, born out of suffering and death, are worthy of respect. Their entrenchment reflects lessons learned from bitter struggle. It demeans that struggle to suggest that the entrenchment should be undone because of fleeting impulses or temporary political pressure.

In a nutshell, this is the argument for why at least some past decisions should take precedence over some current decisions. The argument has been formalized by constitutional theorist Bruce Ackerman, who labels the historical periods producing such decisions "constitutional moments." Ackerman's theory is complex, and I will not rehearse its details here. In particular, there is no reason to tie our discussion to Ackerman's detailed and idiosyncratic ideas about the precise markers of constitutional moments. His main point is that at some dramatic periods in our history, citizens become so mobilized that they transcend ordinary politics and are able to think in a concentrated fashion about the future they envision for their country. Decisions that come out of such periods should be preserved and respected.

It would be foolish to claim that this argument lacks force, and I have tried to present it in the most forceful way possible. Still, there are significant problems with this line of thinking.

First, it seems silly to insist that all the Constitution's detail—the hard-wired minutia—is the product of deep public deliberation by an aroused citizenry. How many deeply aroused citizens focused on the fact that the Fourteenth Amendment excluded "Indians not taxed" from the population when apportioning seats in the House of Representatives? Is it really plausible that many of citizens in 1788 focused on, say, the exact line of succession for the presidency or the precise qualifications for members of the House? Of course, for the same reason that these provisions attracted little attention then, their entrenchment also matters less now. I would not insist that these provisions always present major obstacles to formulation of sound public policy. Still, they sometimes prevent implementation of our own, contemporary preferences, and Ackerman's theory provides no reason for why they should have this effect.

Second, although citizens may pay more attention to the broad outlines of the Constitution and to its amendments at "constitutional moments," they are unlikely to pay any real attention to how these provisions would intersect with future realities. Often, they will not be able to guess what these future realities will be. The constitutional questions that confront us today are not about abstractions, but about how particular controversies should be resolved. Even if the Reconstruction period was a constitutional moment, the public engagement at that time did not extend to whether modern affirmative action plans are constitutionally permissible or to whether same-sex marriage is an aspect of liberty. When we make judgments about these specific issues by interpreting an old and general text, we are not giving effect to decisions made by past, mobilized, and engaged majorities.

Finally, it is a mistake to exaggerate the extent to which constitution writers escape the narrow disputes of their own time and place. Not all constitutional provisions emerge from constitutional moments and much constitutional language is therefore not worthy of this special respect. There was no popular mobilization yanking people out of their ordinary complacency accompanying the enactment of the Twentieth Amendment, which changed the date on which the president assumed office and tinkered with the rules of presidential succession. The rules about presidential disability in the Twenty-Fifth Amendment may or may not be wise, but no one supposes that they were a manifestation of the general will or written by "We the People."

What about constitutional provisions written during more dramatic moments in our history? Although we nurture myths about the "miracle at Philadelphia," or "the battle cry of freedom" during the Civil War, serious historians know that even in times of crisis many political actors remain mired in interest-group politics. As Thomas Jefferson wrote years after the founding period, "I knew that age well; I belonged to it, and labored with it. It deserved well of its country. It was very like the present, but without the experience of the present."

Jefferson's deflationary account of the founding period is more than justified. Ratification of the new Constitution was hardly a foregone conclusion, and it was achieved thanks to a series of backroom deals and appeals to special interests. Many of the Constitution's supporters were motivated by authentic concern for the country, but it is also true that many of them wanted to protect their investment in Revolutionary War debt or, more broadly, to promote the interests of the emerging creditor and manufacturing class against the interests of debtors and farmers. The document that resulted from their efforts involved many special-interest compromises, in particular between the interests of the large and small states and the slave and free states.

The debates about ratification were similarly mired in interest-group politics. Ratification conventions focused on questions like whether navigation along the Mississippi would continue, whether states with seaports would be able to collect revenue from states without them, and whether new states would be formed from existing ones. Sometimes, the issues were even more parochial. For example, without ratification by Massachusetts, the Constitution probably would have been defeated. Massachusetts's ratification, in turn, depended crucially on the support of Governor John Hancock, and Hancock agreed to support the Constitution only after he was promised support for his reelection campaign.

Some of the concerns of the Reconstruction Congress that drafted the Thirteenth, Fourteenth, and Fifteenth Amendments were similarly narrow. The Radical Republicans in control of Congress were authentically motivated by hatred of slavery, but some of them were also racists. Moreover, they had immediate political concerns like preserving their congressional majority in the face of increased southern voting power if the three-fifths compromise were abrogated.

Suppose, though, that we put all this to one side and imagine that all constitutional language is in fact the product of special, constitutional moments. Even on this unrealistic assumption, it is hard to see why we should be obligated to obey past decisions. After all, the very fact that measures were adopted during constitutional moments gives them a built-in advantage when we decide on our current preferences. Even in the absence of a method for binding precommitment, current defenders of such past decisions have a powerful rhetorical tool at their disposal. They can attempt to persuade us, now, that the past decisions are worthy of respect because of the special set of historical events that led to them. This is the very tool I utilized at the beginning of this section when I described why one might think that the Reconstruction Amendments are entitled to special respect.

The question we need to confront is why we should be bound by these past decisions in cases when we are no longer persuaded of their wisdom in our world. A specific example neatly makes the point. It is only happenstance that the original Thirteenth Amendment, which would have entrenched slavery, was not enacted. Both Houses of Congress adopted the amendment by the requisite two-thirds supermajority, and there is little reason to doubt that it would have been ratified by a sufficient number of state legislatures if the war had not broken out. With the nation teetering on the edge of disunion and the entire country mobilized over the question of secession, it seems clear that the amendment would have been adopted at a "constitutional moment." Yet it is hard to see why, even if it had been adopted, we today should be bound by such an egregiously wrong decision. We can, today, appreciate the historical circumstances that led to the amendment but also choose as a matter of our modern views to reject it. Indeed, the very refusal to be bound by this precommitment might be seen as constituting the current United States as a political community.

COMMUNITY AND TIME

This last observation brings us to the question of what in fact constitutes us as a political community extending over time. As I have suggested, the precommitment strategy depends on the analogy between autonomy-friendly individual precommitment and national precommitment. But it is far from obvious that the analogy holds.

When Ahab tells his crew to ignore his own future demand to stop the procedure, it seems natural to assume that it is the same Ahab who gives both directives. Perhaps even this is an illusion. Perhaps even individual identity does not extend over time. It is much more problematic, though, to claim that the particular individuals who attended ratifying conventions in the late 1780s are the same people who are bound by their work several centuries later. For Thomas Jefferson, a different analogy better captured the relationship between past and present. He wrote that "one generation is to another as one independent nation to another." If this is the more apt analogy, then national precommitment is hardly an exercise in freedom. Instead, it amounts to intergenerational imperialism.

The fragility of the analogy between individual people, on the one hand, and separate generations, on the other, should be a problem for constitutionalists, but, oddly, some of them have cleverly turned it into an argument for their position. In a brilliant and deeply learned book, Yale Law Professor Jed Rubenfeld seizes on Jefferson's insight and makes it face in the opposite direction. Precisely because we see the United States as an ongoing entity—precisely because America's past is not an "independent nation" to us—we are collectively bound to our earlier decisions in just the way that individuals are bound to theirs.

Put differently, Rubenfeld takes what I have described as an anxiety and turns it into an argument. An individual who thought of himself as becoming a different person with each passing moment would quickly go crazy. For that very reason, Rubenfeld argues, present individual decisions are influenced not by *precommitment* but by *commitment*. On this account, the point is not that the individual has actually bound herself and limited her freedom at some prior time. Committed individuals are not bound to the mast. Instead, they make a present, free choice to honor their past decisions. By doing so, they give meaning, direction, and unity to their lives. Indeed, Rubenfeld insists, what it means to be free is to integrate present choices with some past set of commitments.

So, too, on Rubenfeld's account, a nation that tries to live only in the present risks a kind of collective unraveling. What makes us a nation—what differentiates the United States from Mexico—is a political order that extends over time. As Rubenfeld puts it, "Democratic self-government is ... something that exists, if it exists at all, only over time. ... [D]emocracy consists not in governance by the present will of the governed, or in governance by the a-temporal truths posted by one or another moral philosopher, but rather in a people's living out its own self-given political and legal commitments over time—apart from or even contrary to popular will at any given moment."

It is tempting to dismiss Rubenfeld's argument as an example of what the great twentieth-century lawyer Felix Cohen once called "transcendental nonsense." Cohen was a follower of Oliver Wendell Holmes, and at the dawn of modern American legal thought, Holmes instructed us that "[w]e must think things not words, or at least we must constantly translate our words into the facts for which they stand, if we are to keep to the real and the true."

Instead of "thinking things," Rubenfeld seems to be in the thrall of metaphysical abstraction. Whatever the status of individual commitments, the notion of collective, national commitments seems divorced from anything that actually exists in the world. There were, after all, real individual people in Philadelphia in 1787, and all of those real people are now really dead. There are, today, real people who are alive and who must decide how to solve real, modern problems. One might suppose that a sensible way to solve those problems would be to make all-things-considered judgments about what is to be done. Instead, Rubenfeld wants us to focus on "self-given political and legal commitments over time," an abstraction rather than a thing. I understand that if I made a promise in the past, the same "I" who is alive now has an obligation to live up to that promise. But I made no promise in Philadelphia. I did not sign their document or participate in their deliberations. If we focus on concrete reality rather than metaphysical abstraction, it is easy to see that their promises are not my promises.

As I will argue below, appreciation of the artificiality of collective commitment over time helps to solve the problem of constitutional obligation. It is too facile, though, to claim that this focus completely refutes Rubenfeld's position. Collective identity over time may be "transcendental nonsense," but it does not follow that it is possible to both free ourselves from this "nonsense" and retain our sanity. Cohen and Holmes sometimes seem to assume that we can somehow appreciate reality without any artificial mediating structures that organize and make sense of the external world. But our understanding of the external world is inevitably mediated by such structures. Without them, we would be bombarded by a riot of random and meaningless sense perceptions. We would, indeed, go crazy. Perhaps these perceptions would not be "transcendental," but, without some method of organizing them, they would surely be "nonsense." Abstract "metaphysical" structures of thought ward off, rather than cause, the perception of nonsense.

One structure that makes sense of the world is the category "The United States of America." One can imagine a utopian world where we no longer had need of this artificial category—where we believed in and acted on the principle that there was no distinction between, say, citizens of Mexico and citizens of the United States. The great philosopher Derek Parfit has argued that we might in similar fashion someday overcome the illusion that we as individuals are separate from other individuals. But, intriguing as they are, these possibilities are utopian. If we are to think real things, then one real thing in the here and now is that people are not presently capable of perceiving the world this way. Instead, there is a category of "me" and a category of "The United States of America." And Rubenfeld is right that if we are to make any sense at all of these categories, they must be understood to extend over time.

The hard question, though, is what precisely follows from this insight. For Rubenfeld, what follows is that we have an obligation to respect the national commitments that the constructed "we" made years ago when "we" ratified the United States Constitution. But this is a non sequitur, or, at least, so it seems to me. Because these categories are constructed—because they are heuristics that we use to organize and make sense of the world rather than the world itself—we have an ongoing choice between structures.

Once we see that we have a choice, the possibility emerges that the people alive at any one time will make different choices. In other words, it becomes plain that constitutionalism is a site for struggle and contestation rather than for settlement. There is disagreement about how to make sense of our own history. One might embrace a national narrative emphasizing ongoing commitment to a set of norms established in

1789 and working themselves pure through several centuries of elaboration and interpretation. But one might also embrace a narrative that emphasizes struggle and dissension. On this view, the defining characteristic of our political order is precisely that the political order is never finally defined. For someone who organizes our history in this fashion, Americans are always straining against prior commitments rather than placidly embracing them. On this view, constitutional disobedience is not only permissible; it is built into the fabric of our country.

Depending on which organizing heuristic one adopts, different moments in our history are crucial and different historical figures are iconic. Whereas one camp celebrates George Washington magisterially presiding over the constitutional convention, the other celebrates Thomas Jefferson's insistence that "the earth belongs to the living" and his decision to purchase the Louisiana Territory despite his own view that the purchase was unconstitutional. One camp points to pre–Civil War lawyers like Alvan Stewart who argued before unsympathetic judges that slavery was unconstitutional. The other points to abolitionist William Lloyd Garrison's brave assertion that the Constitution was "a covenant with death and an agreement with hell." One camp honors the Supreme Court's stubborn insistence on constitutional principle in the face of massive resistance to its decision in *Brown v. Board of Education*. The other honors Justice Robert Jackson's statements to his fellow justices while they were considering *Brown* where he expressed his willingness to join the result because of moral and political imperatives even though, in his view, the Constitution did not support the outcome.

If the second view is correct, then Rubenfeld's image of commitment over time eats its own tail. The very commitment that we as a political community have lived out is a commitment to openness, rebellion, and a continual straining against the yoke.

But is the second view correct? The question is at once misleading and dispositive. It is misleading because it assumes that there is a right and wrong to the choice of the heuristic by which we organize our experience of the world. But because the heuristic is something that we impose on the world rather than the world itself, talking about right and wrong in this context is a category mistake.

The question is also dispositive because it brings to the surface the possibility of choice. A commitment view ultimately rests on the notion that national identity is not chosen, or at least not chosen *now*. As Rubenfeld explicitly argues, commitments are lived over time, not willed at a particular moment. As soon as one admits that there is a choice—that we might use a different heuristic and define our national identity in a different way—then it becomes difficult or impossible to eradicate the nagging possibility of choice from our consciousness.

It is for just this reason that the question of constitutional obedience is absent from our discourse. The Constitution's defenders cannot admit the possibility of disobedience, for to do so is already to lose the argument. If such a thing is possible—if there really is a choice whether or not to obey—then there can no longer be political order that rests on the inevitability of submission to the past. Once we see that the past has a hold on us only if we let it, the hold immediately loosens.

And so we are confronted with a conspiracy of fearful silence. But the Constitution's defenders cannot keep the possibility of freedom a secret from us forever. The subversive truth need only be spoken and our chains begin to fall away.

CHAPTER THREE

...

The Banality of Constitutional Violation

MANY PEOPLE THINK that a country without a constitution would be a very scary place. We may disagree in fundamental ways about the kind of society we want to live in, but no one wants our civic life to devolve into complete chaos. It is doubtless the fear of such chaos that helps cement an otherwise very diverse coalition favoring constitutional obedience.

Is the fear justified? In previous chapters, I have made theoretical arguments for why I think that it is not. A fair response to these arguments is that when it comes to the possibility of a war of all against all, we ought to be very risk averse. We cannot know for sure what would happen if we dramatically changed the nature of political obligation, and we ought to think long and hard about radical experiments that could end in disaster.

In this chapter, I attempt to respond to these concerns. My argument is that we do not need to speculate about a world with widespread constitutional violation because this is the world in which we already live. As things stand now, government officials, high and low, routinely violate the Constitution, and no one does anything about it. Yet the last time I looked, things seemed pretty normal. I did not notice fighting in the streets, rampant lawlessness, or a return to a state of nature.

There is an immediate obstacle to proving, rather than merely asserting, the existence of widespread constitutional violation. The problem is that there is fundamental disagreement about how to interpret the Constitution. Different people believe that we should glean the Constitution's meaning from the text as originally understood, from the text as understood today in light of contemporary conditions, from the intent of the framers, from our traditions, from the gradual accretion of constitutional doctrine, from our commitment to democracy, and even from moral and political philosophy. The upshot is that any example I might provide of constitutional violation is likely to be met by someone insisting that, given her interpretive commitments, it is instead an example of constitutional fidelity.

To be sure, there are some cases where almost everyone would agree that the Constitution has been or should be ignored. For example, Article I makes the vice president the presiding officer of the Senate, but provides that when the president is tried for an impeachable offense, the chief justice shall preside. This language pretty clearly means that the vice president should preside over his own impeachment. As it happens, there has never been an impeachment trial of a vice president, but I am confident that if there ever is one, someone else will serve as the presiding officer. The framers were very wise men, but they were not perfect, and it was, after all, a very long, hot summer in Philadelphia. They were bound to make mistakes, and this is surely one. Almost everyone, I think, would agree that we should simply ignore it.

We don't have to speculate about our willingness to ignore other mistakes. For example, the Constitution mandates that when new states are added to the Union, both of the initial senators serve a term of six years. Nonetheless, ever since Vermont joined the United States as the first new state in 1791, the provision has been routinely violated. One new senator from a new state has always been assigned a term of less than six years in order to provide for staggered senatorial elections. During the debate over the admission of Alaska as a new state, a back-bench Senator had the poor judgment to violate our conspiracy of silence on this matter. He pointed out the obvious discrepancy between the constitutional language and our practices. The manager of the bill quickly replied that this was the way things had always been done, and the question was abruptly dropped.

These examples are important because they demonstrate that even when the text is very clear, it is possible to disobey specific provisions of the Constitution without dire consequences. The structure of our civil order has not crumbled.

By themselves, however, these examples do not demonstrate systematic or widespread violation or put to rest fears of what such violations would entail. To meet those fears, we need to find a way to determine how often the Constitution has been violated without becoming enmeshed in controversial questions about how it should be interpreted. In the rest of this chapter, I suggest a number of techniques we can use to provide a rough measure of the extent of constitutional disobedience even in the face of unresolved disputes over what should count as disobedience.

INTERPRETIVE DISAGREEMENT

Ironically, the very fact of interpretive disagreement provides one tool for abstracting from them. Major decisions by the Supreme Court that have had a profound effect on our constitutional culture have utilized very different and conflicting methodologies. For example, when the Supreme Court held that the Constitution guaranteed the right to individual gun ownership in *District of Columbia v. Heller*, it carefully parsed the individual words of the Second Amendment and examined how those words were used and understood at the time the amendment was written. In contrast, when the Court invalidated racial segregation in public education in *Brown v. Board of Education*, it found that originalist sources were "not enough to resolve the problem with which we are faced." After observing that "we cannot turn the clock back to 1868 when the [Fourteenth Amendment] was adopted," it focused on "public education in the light of its full development and its present place in American life throughout the Nation." At least the *Brown* Court anchored its holding in specific constitutional text—the equal protection clause of the Fourteenth Amendment. But when the Court held that women had a fundamental right to an abortion in *Roe v. Wade*, it conceded that "[t]he Constitution does not explicitly mention any right of privacy," and made no more than casual and passing reference to constitutional text.

As if these disputes were not bad enough, even when there is agreement about methodology, reasonable people disagree about the application of the methodology. Both the majority opinion and the dissents in *Heller* purported to be guided by the original understanding of the Second Amendment, yet the justices on each side reached radically different results.

Given this kind of fundamental disagreement, it is not surprising that dissenting justices regularly claim that their colleagues have engaged in egregious constitutional violations. When the Court held in *Miranda v. Arizona* that the Fifth Amendment privilege against self-incrimination mandated that suspects be warned of their right to remain silent before custodial interrogation, Justice John Harlan wrote in dissent that "[n]othing in the letter or the spirit of the Constitution or in the precedents squares with the heavy-handed and one-sided action that is so precipitously taken by the Court in the name of fulfilling its constitutional responsibilities." When the Court reversed its own precedent to permit "victim impact statements" in capital cases, Justice Thurgood Marshall wrote that "[p]ower, not reason, is the new currency of this Court's decisionmaking." When the Supreme Court handed the presidency to George W. Bush, Justice John Paul Stevens complained that his colleagues had lent "credence to the most cynical appraisal of the work of judges throughout the land," and that they had damaged "the Nation's confidence in the judge as an impartial guardian of the rule of law." And when the Supreme Court struck down a state measure discriminating against gay men and lesbians, Justice Antonin Scalia wrote that "[t]oday's opinion has no foundation in American constitutional law, and barely pretends to."

No doubt, at least some of these statements are hyperbolic. Moreover, without committing ourselves to a particular interpretive method, we cannot know which of these decisions in fact does conflict with the Constitution. Nonetheless, the examples illustrate two important points. First, many of the justices themselves seem to believe that important Supreme Court decisions amount to serious constitutional violations. Second, even if we cannot know *which* cases involve violations, we can be certain that *some* of them do. Because the Court's various interpretive methods are irreconcilable, some of the results generated by some of the methods must be wrong.

It is important to note the limits of my argument. My claim here is not that anyone has deliberately disobeyed the Constitution. Later in this chapter, I will discuss some cases of deliberate disobedience. For now, though, we can assume that these examples of interpretive disagreement are among people who, in good faith, are trying their best to comply with the Constitution's commands. These disagreements nonetheless establish that someone, some of the time, is violating the Constitution in the sense that he or she is taking actions inconsistent with its requirements as properly understood.

These are not minor errors. Cases like *Heller, Brown, Miranda*, and *Roe* are central to our constitutional culture. They govern broad areas of our national life and provide core examples of judicial enforcement of constitutional principles. Given this fact, it is ironic that they also conclusively demonstrate the centrality of constitutional violation.

A similar argument is rooted in the Court's overruling of important precedent. For example, *Brown* overruled *Plessy v. Ferguson*, which for over a half century permitted state-mandated segregation. In *Mapp v. Ohio*, the Court reversed years of precedent that permitted state courts to utilize illegally seized evidence. And in a series of cases decided after 1937, the Court overruled many of its decisions striking down regulatory and redistributive legislation. Once again, for present purposes it is unnecessary to decide whether the initial decisions were wrong or whether the decisions overruling them were mistaken. Either way, it is plain that the country successfully endured years of constitutional violations relating to important constitutional principles.

Perhaps some of these dramatic reversals might be explained by the fact that underlying social conditions evolved in ways that somehow changed constitutional requirements. For example, as already noted, the *Brown* Court relied upon the dramatically changed status of public education when it overruled *Plessy*. On some (but certainly not all) interpretive theories, these changed circumstances might mean that both *Plessy* and *Brown* were correctly decided.

But there are less dramatic changes that resist this explanation. For example, within very short periods of time, the Court has reversed course on whether the Constitution protects the right to secure certain kinds of late-term abortions and on whether various sorts of campaign-finance regulation are constitutional. The Court's inability to settle on an approach to the Tenth Amendment provides another, especially embarrassing, example. At first blush, the Tenth Amendment seems to state no more than a truism. It provides that "[t]he powers not delegated to the United States by the Constitution, nor prohibited by it to the States, are reserved to the States respectively, or to the people." As a textual matter, this language seems to mean only that if the federal government tries to do something that is not authorized by one of its enumerated powers (like, say, the power to regulate interstate commerce or the power to declare and wage war), then it has acted unconstitutionally.

Despite this textual impediment, the Court has experimented with various additional limitations on federal power said to be implied by the Tenth Amendment. In *National League of Cities v. Usery*, decided in 1976, the Court held that the Tenth Amendment prohibited the federal government from regulating the states "in areas of traditional governmental functions," even though the regulation otherwise fell within the commerce clause power. For the next ten years, the Court rendered a series of confusing and inconsistent opinions attempting to apply this new principle. Then, in 1985, in *Garcia v. San Antonio Metropolitan Transit Authority*, the justices announced that it had all been a mistake, that the *National League of Cities* test was "unworkable," and that the case was overruled.

Not satisfied with this outcome either, the justices made a new attempt to define limits implicit in the Tenth Amendment in *New York v. United States*, decided in 1992. *New York* held that in certain circumstances, efforts to "commandeer" state governments were unconstitutional. Predictably, this test also led to confusion, and now the Court seems to have cut back on it, at least to some extent, as well.

These embarrassing reversals, all of which occurred in a roughly fifteen-year period, cannot be explained by dramatically changed circumstances. Rather, they result from changes in membership of the Court and changes of heart by some of the justices. We need not take sides in the ongoing dispute about the constitutional scope of federal power to see that some of these decisions must necessarily represent departures from constitutional commands.

DELIBERATE DEPARTURES

To be sure, these are cases where the justices were at least presumptively *trying* to obey the Constitution. They involve good-faith departures from constitutional requirements, not outright defiance. No one has unmediated access to the Constitution, so mistakes are inevitable. The persistence and inevitability of mistakes do establish that the worst fears of the Constitution's defenders will not be realized. They show that departures—even frequent and serious departures—from the Constitution's commands do not produce chaos. Still, one might differentiate between good-faith mistakes, on the one hand, and deliberate disobedience, on the other. Even if mistakes alone do not cause an unraveling of our civic peace, perhaps deliberate disobedience would.

In other situations, though, the justices have deliberately departed from their own conceptions of what the Constitution requires. Consider, for example, the case of Justice Robert Jackson. During his confirmation hearings, Chief Justice John Roberts named Jackson as one of the former justices he most admired. By itself, the choice of Jackson was no surprise. Although he is not as famous as some of his colleagues, Jackson, who served from 1941 until his death in 1954, is widely respected by many students of the Supreme Court. What is more surprising is that Roberts would have chosen Jackson in light of the way Roberts otherwise presented himself during the hearings.

Roberts famously testified that Supreme Court justices were analogous to baseball umpires calling balls and strikes. His point was that justices should merely follow the law and not allow their personal opinions to color their legal judgment. Given his "balls and strikes" argument, Roberts' admiration for Jackson is more than a little puzzling. In fact, Jackson, perhaps more forcefully and frequently than any other justice, made clear his belief that there were times when the Constitution, even as he best understood it, should be ignored.

Three of the most important cases decided during Jackson's tenure illustrate the point. During World War II, the Roosevelt administration forcibly evacuated Americans of Japanese descent from the West Coast and put them in what amounted to concentration camps in the interior. In *Korematsu v. United States*, the Supreme Court upheld the constitutionality of the evacuation. Justice Jackson dissented, but only because he thought that it was wrong to involve the court system in conduct that seemed to him to be unconstitutional. He made it very clear that he did not object to the unconstitutional conduct itself.

> It would be impracticable and dangerous idealism to expect or insist that each specific military command in an area of probable operations will conform to conventional tests of constitutionality. When an area is so beset that it must be put under military control at all, the paramount consideration is that its measures be successful, rather than legal.

Some eight years later, during the Korean War, President Truman ordered the seizure of the nation's steel mills in order to avoid a strike. In an opinion by Justice Black, the Supreme Court held that the seizure was unconstitutional. Black's opinion purported to do no more than apply constitutional text. Jackson agreed that the president's actions should be invalidated, but his much more famous and justly celebrated opinion took a very different approach. He noted that

> A judge...may be surprised at the poverty of really useful and unambiguous authority applicable to concrete problems of executive power as they actually present themselves. Just what our forefathers did envision, or would have envisioned had they foreseen modern conditions, must be divined from materials almost as enigmatic as the dreams Joseph was called upon to interpret for Pharaoh.

In at least some situations, Jackson thought, the result should turn on "the imperatives of events and contemporary imponderables rather than on abstract theories of law."

Finally, in the last year of his life, Jackson participated in deliberations over *Brown v. Board of Education*. Like all of his colleagues, he signed Chief Justice Warren's opinion invalidating public school segregation. After his death, however, records of the justices' private deliberations were made public, and we now know what Jackson really thought. Jackson told his colleagues that

> This is a political question. To me personally, this is not a problem....
>
> As a political decision, I can go along with it but with a protest that it is politics.

In a draft concurrence, which he ultimately decided not to publish, he wrote that "[c]onvenient as it would be to reach an opposite conclusion, I simply cannot find in the conventional material of constitutional interpretation any justification for saying that in maintaining segregated schools any state or the District of Columbia can be judicially decreed, up to the date of this decision, to have violated the Fourteenth Amendment."

In each of these cases, Justice Jackson, by his own account, endorsed or participated in actions that he thought unconstitutional. He thought the test for military action was that it be "successful" whether or not it was "legal," that the legitimacy of presidential power should sometimes be determined by "the imperatives of events" rather than "abstract theories of law," and that the Supreme Court itself should exceed its constitutional authority by invalidating state segregation laws even though the laws were constitutionally permissible. Given this record, it says something significant about American constitutional culture that Jackson is so widely revered, even by jurists like Chief Justice Roberts who purport to believe in judicial restraint and the supremacy of the Constitution.

Nor is Jackson alone in embracing constitutional disobedience. For example, we know from their conference notes that during the period of "massive resistance" to school desegregation, on more than one occasion, the Supreme Court departed from what the justices believed were the commands of the Constitution because of a political judgment about what would happen if those commands were enforced. And in our own time, even as thoroughgoing an originalist as Justice Scalia has conceded that if his study of constitutional material convinced him that public flogging was not prohibited by the original understanding, he would nonetheless vote to invalidate it.

Moreover, even if the Supreme Court always obeyed the Constitution as the justices best understood it, we would still have to contend with disobedience by other political actors. Some of our most revered presidents have expressed a willingness to violate constitutional commands. For example, Thomas Jefferson negotiated the Louisiana Purchase even though he had the gravest of doubts as to its constitutionality. At the beginning of the Civil War, Abraham Lincoln unilaterally suspended the writ of habeas corpus and then ignored a decision by the chief justice of the United States requiring the release of a prisoner. Lincoln evidently believed that most, if not all, of his actions were constitutional, but his public statements about the matters are at least susceptible to the interpretation that he thought the actions were justified even if unconstitutional. In an address to Congress, he posed the rhetorical question, "Are all the laws, but one, to go unexecuted, and the government itself go to pieces, lest that one be violated?"

The decisions by Jefferson and Lincoln were high profile and controversial. Unremedied constitutional violations by lower level officials occur much more frequently. Most legal issues do not reach the Supreme Court, and the Court has promulgated a web of doctrine that ensures that some issues cannot be decided by any court. Rules as diverse as the political question doctrine, the mootness, ripeness, and standing requirements, the state secrets privilege, and various forms of sovereign and official immunity prevent courts from adjudicating many important constitutional questions. These doctrines have the effect of giving political actors authority to obey or disobey the Constitution as they choose.

How do political actors use this discretion? Some no doubt attempt to follow the dictates of the Constitution to the best of their abilities, but some assuredly do not. Consider, for example, the problem of partisan gerrymandering. A plurality of the Supreme Court has ruled that the partisan gerrymander presents a political question that is not justiciable. Importantly, it does not follow from this holding that the Supreme Court thinks the practice is constitutional. Rather, it has held only that the lack of judicially manageable standards prevents the Court from adjudicating the question.

Freed from judicial oversight and with the aid of sophisticated computer programs, state legislators regularly and egregiously manipulate district lines for nakedly partisan purposes. No one who knows anything about the practice imagines that most of these legislators are conscientiously thinking about constitutional constraints as they go about this dubious work. Instead, at least in this instance, the Supreme Court's refusal to provide judicial enforcement of constitutional commands means that there is no enforcement at all. The predictable result is constitutional disobedience.

DEPARTMENTALISM

Paradoxically, constitutional disobedience can also arise when political actors think of themselves as following the commands of the Constitution. Consider, for example, the case of Chief Judge Roy Moore of the Alabama Supreme Court. Judge Moore ordered the installation of a mammoth monument to the Ten Commandments in the lobby of a state court building. When a federal court ordered him to dismantle the monument, he refused. A state ethics panel thereupon ordered his removal from office. According to William Thompson, the head of the panel, Thompson and his colleagues had little choice because "the chief justice placed himself above the law" by defying a federal court order.

At first, one might think that, as Thompson supposed, the disciplining of Chief Judge Moore amounts to a vindication of the rule of law and of constitutional governance. In fact, though, viewed from Judge Moore's perspective, it demonstrates something close to the opposite. One does not have to agree with Judge Moore to see the irony of Thompson's statement. The "law" that one should be subservient to is presumably the Constitution itself, not a federal judge's erroneous opinion about what the Constitution says. Of course, if the federal judge was right, then respect for his decision counts as constitutional obedience. But if the federal judge was wrong—and Judge Moore thought that he was wrong—then Judge Moore was complying with the Constitution even though he was disobeying the federal judge's erroneous order.

Importantly, the panel that removed Judge Moore from office did not reach a conclusion as to whether the federal court had decided the case correctly. Apparently, then, the panel thought that Judge Moore's removal from office was appropriate even if it was Judge Moore, rather than the federal judge, who best understood the Constitution.

It is clear why the ethics panel ruled in the way it did. The worry is that if everyone could decide for themselves what the Constitution meant, there would be complete chaos. This worry, in turn, suggests that the standard argument for constitutional obedience has things backward. The usual argument is that without the Constitution, there would be anarchy, but it is actually fidelity to the Constitution that risks producing this result. If every actor were obliged or permitted to obey his best understanding of the Constitution, there would be no hierarchical, orderly system for resolving our disputes. *Constitutional* obedience would produce widespread *civil* disobedience. Anyone who thought that any statute was unconstitutional would feel free to disobey the statute because of her obligation to obey the Constitution.

Proponents of hierarchical order argue that this is an intolerable state of affairs. They claim with considerable force that if we are to have a workable government, there must be a method by which constitutional disagreement is authoritatively resolved. What they do not always recognize is that such a resolution necessarily means that for the sake of public order, individual actors will have to give up on their obligation to obey the Constitution as they best understand it.

Of course, this outcome is unproblematic in cases where these understandings are incorrect. If Judge Moore misunderstood the Constitution, then it is possible to satisfy both the requirement of constitutional fidelity and the requirement of hierarchical order. A problem arises, though, in cases where actors like Judge Moore correctly understand the meaning of the Constitution. Then the two requirements conflict, and we face the question of whether constitutional obedience should be subordinated. The ethics panel that removed Judge Moore from office clearly thought that constitutional obedience was less important than hierarchical order. It held that Judge Moore was obligated to obey the District Court's order even if that order was inconsistent with the Constitution.

The United States Supreme Court has held much the same thing even in cases where it is undisputed that the constitutional interpretation is erroneous. For example, in *Walker v. City of Birmingham*, the Court assumed arguendo that an injunction prohibiting certain civil rights demonstrations violated the Constitution, yet it held that on the facts of that case, demonstrators were nonetheless obligated to obey it and that it was appropriate to jail them for violating a putatively unconstitutional order. Similarly, the Court has repeatedly stated that lower courts are required to obey Supreme Court precedent even when the Supreme Court itself thinks that the precedent is erroneous and should be overruled. As Justice Scalia recently summarized the law, the Supreme Court has

always held that "it is this Court's prerogative alone to overrule one of its precedents."... That has been true even where "'changes in

judicial doctrine' ha[ve] significantly undermined" our prior holding,..., and even where our prior holding "appears to rest on reasons rejected in some other line of decisions."

None of this would be much of a problem if the Constitution itself required that its substantive commands be subordinated to hierarchical
order. If the Constitution provided that, say, the substantive right to
freedom of speech could be abrogated by a Supreme Court decision
that incorrectly interpreted the First Amendment's substantive commands, then the requirements of constitutional fidelity and hierarchical
order would not conflict. I address this possibility below. Before getting
to it, though, we need to explore the potential conflict between the two
goals in greater detail.

Suppose that Congress or the president thinks that obedience to
their oaths to support and defend the Constitution requires action that
is inconsistent with what the Supreme Court has said. Should they
nonetheless obey the Supreme Court? Some scholars have argued in
favor of what has come to be called "departmentalism"—the position
that each department of government has the right to insist upon its
own interpretation of the Constitution.

Departmentalism comes in different forms, some of which are more
radical than others. In its mildest form, departmentalism means that
the executive and legislative branches should make their own constitutional judgments when they are exercising their independent legitimate
powers that are not subject to judicial review. For example, even if Supreme Court precedent establishes that a particular piece of legislation
is within Congress's enumerated powers, an individual congressman
might vote against the law because he takes a narrower view of those
powers. Perhaps it is appropriate as well for him to vote in favor of a law
that takes a broader view of his powers than the Supreme Court would
take. Similarly, a president might veto a law because he believes it to be
unconstitutional even though it is clear that the Supreme Court would

uphold the statute and might sign a law that he knows the Supreme Court will invalidate. Judge Brett Cavenaugh, a judge on the United States Court of Appeals for the District of Columbia Circuit, has endorsed this form of departmentalism with respect to President Obama's health care law. He wrote that "[u]nder the Constitution, the president may decline to enforce a statute that regulates private individuals when the president deems the statute unconstitutional, even if a court has held or would hold the statute constitutional."

A more aggressive form of departmentalism holds that Supreme Court decisions bind the particular parties to the case, but do not bind other actors, who remain free to read the Constitution differently even in a case exactly analogous to the case the Court has decided. Lincoln took this position with regard to the *Dred Scott* decision, which struck down a congressional prohibition on slavery in the territories. Lincoln conceded that the decision determined the status of Dred Scott himself, but claimed that the president and Congress remained entitled to act on their own views with regard to territorial slavery more generally. Much more recently, then–Attorney General Edwin Meese argued for this position during the Reagan administration. And with regard to lower court decisions, the executive branch frequently refuses to acquiesce to United States Court of Appeals decisions when dealing with cases in other circuits.

At the height of "massive resistance" to *Brown v. Board of Education*, many southern officials embraced this form of departmentalism. They claimed that they were not obligated to follow *Brown* unless ordered to do so in a specific case. In *Cooper v. Aaron*, a case growing out of the effort to desegregate the Little Rock public schools, the Supreme Court rejected this position and announced that its decisions bound all government officials. It should be obvious that *Cooper* cannot end the controversy, however. As discussed in more detail below, a departmentalist might well claim that other government officials are entitled to disagree with the Supreme Court about *Cooper* itself.

The third version of departmentalism is the most radical. It holds that government officials are entitled to act on their own view of the Constitution even when the Supreme Court announces a contrary view in the very case in dispute. Today, there are not many defenders of this position. Richard Nixon explicitly declined to assert this power when he acquiesced to a Supreme Court decision ordering him to turn over incriminating tape recordings of Oval Office conversations. Similarly, Harry Truman obeyed a Supreme Court order requiring him to return to private ownership steel mills that he had ordered seized to prevent a strike.

It is worth remembering, though, that some of our most revered presidents acted or threatened to act on this radical form of departmentalism. Thomas Jefferson made clear that he would not obey an order that would have directed his secretary of state to deliver a judicial commission to a magistrate appointed by his predecessor, John Adams. (In *Marbury v. Madison*, the Court ended up not issuing the order after finding that it lacked jurisdiction over the case). Abraham Lincoln refused to follow a decision written by Chief Justice Roger Taney that required him to release a federal prisoner. When it appeared that the Supreme Court might invalidate legislation canceling "gold clauses" in contracts, Franklin Roosevelt made contingency plans to resist the Court's decision—plans he never acted upon because the Court ended up upholding the statute. Similarly, he threatened to convene a military tribunal and execute German saboteurs even if the Supreme Court ordered him not to do so.

Despite these precedents, departmentalism remains at best a deviant strand in American constitutional jurisprudence. For the most part, and in most contexts, legal scholars and the general public alike accept judicial supremacy on issues of constitutional law. Indeed, judicial supremacy has come to be seen as the same thing as "the rule of law." It is therefore important to point out that it is not the same thing at all. Instead, judicial supremacy embodies the rule of order. We accept judicial supremacy because in some situations, we cannot have both law and order. Defenders of judicial supremacy correctly point out that without it, we risk a chaotic multitude of conflicting constitutional interpretations. With it, however, we require members of other departments of government to violate their oath to "support and defend the Constitution of the United States."

There is a response to this argument. Order and constitutional obedience might be reconciled if the Constitution itself establishes preference for decisional hierarchy over fidelity to its substantive commands. Some advocates of judicial supremacy claim that the Constitution indeed establishes such a hierarchy and gives conclusive weight to Supreme Court decisions. If the Constitution itself mandates obedience to the Supreme Court, then it is departmentalism, rather than deference to the Supreme Court, that amounts to constitutional disobedience.

Why, though, should we think that the Constitution does mandate judicial supremacy? Sometimes, supporters of judicial supremacy seem to reason backward. Instead of starting with constitutional language, they start with the premise that the Constitution should not be interpreted so as to produce chaos. Because the lack of a definitive method for resolving constitutional disputes would produce chaos, it follows that the Constitution must contain such a method.

It should be obvious that this is no more than another version of the move that sidesteps rather than solves the riddle of constitutional obedience. One might, or course, read the Constitution "pragmatically" so as to provide that whenever obedience to its substantive commands yields strongly distasteful results, the commands can be ignored. This approach is neatly captured in Justice Jackson's famous dictum that the Bill of Rights is not "a suicide pact" or Justice Scalia's more recent assertion that in some cases "common sense" should shape the law.

It is also apparent that if the Constitution in fact permits us to ignore its substantive commands whenever "common sense" requires otherwise, then the temptation to disobey is sharply reduced. The problem, though, is that precisely to the extent that we read the Constitution to provide this flexibility, the requirement of obedience also becomes less meaningful. It is worth emphasizing again that obedience takes hold only when the Constitution demands that we do something that we would not otherwise want to do. If the Constitution instructs us to do only things that we would do anyway, then it does not change any results. The requirement of constitutional obedience therefore does no work.

Suppose, though, that one reads the anti-departmentalist argument as grounded in more than disguised pragmatism. Is it possible to somehow wring the idea of judicial supremacy from the usual techniques of constitutional construction without relying on the assumption that the Constitution means whatever our "common sense" tells us it should mean?

Unfortunately, an argument along these lines is quite implausible. There is no clear constitutional text or statements by the founders supporting this view. If the framers had been asked to endorse this doctrine explicitly, it seems unlikely that they would have voted for a provision expressly stating that all political actors must obey erroneous Supreme Court decisions. What this provision would amount to is a grant of authority to a majority of Supreme Court justices to unilaterally amend the Constitution. We should require compelling textual evidence before assuming that the framers endorsed such a radical view.

In any event, almost everyone rejects departmentalist reasoning even in cases where almost everyone would also agree that the Constitution does not prohibit departmentalism. Suppose, for example, a state supreme court decides a federal constitutional question in a manner that a state trial court believes to be incorrect. Plainly the federal Constitution has nothing to say about the decision-making hierarchy as between levels of the state judiciary. Yet I think almost everyone would agree that the state trial court is obliged to follow the ruling of the state supreme court even though this ruling mandates violation of the federal

Constitution as the state trial judge best understands it. This is an example of preference for hierarchical order over substantive constitutional requirements in a case where the Constitution says nothing about hierarchical order.

Of course, the paradox of departmentalism arises only if we assume that the putatively authoritative interpreter of the Constitution is wrong. If we start by stipulating the "right answer" to constitutional questions, then departmentalism may or may not involve disobedience depending on whether the Court or an executive or legislative official has the "right answer." Perhaps the departmentalism problem can be solved by making a generalization about who is most likely to have the right answer. But this solution once again founders on the problem of constitutional disagreement. Because we cannot agree on what the Constitution means, we also cannot agree on the institutional structures most likely to produce correct interpretations.

All of this leaves us with a dilemma. If departmentalism is accepted, we will have to deal with the very sort of chaos that constitutionalists want to avoid. If it is rejected, the upshot is that some government officials will have to disobey the Constitution as they understand it. It turns out that it is this disobedience that preserves civic peace.

CONSTITUTIONAL REMEDIES AND STARE DECISIS

At least we might take solace from the fact that the rejection of departmentalism leaves the Supreme Court itself free to obey the Constitution as the justices best understand it. In other cases, though, the justices have built constitutional disobedience into the very doctrines that they have promulgated. The two main examples here are remedies for constitutional violations and the doctrine of stare decisis.

With regard to remedies, consider the Fourth Amendment exclusionary rule. For half a century, the Supreme Court has insisted that, at least in some instances, evidence secured as a result of an unconstitutional search must not be used at trial. In recent years, the Court has substantially narrowed the scope of the rule, but it has yet to abandon it.

One reason the modern Court has sharply limited the rule is because it has come to see that the rule does not provide a "remedy" in anything like the usual sense of the word. A remedy is typically designed to compensate the victim for an injury by putting a victim back in the position he would have been in if the injury had not occurred. For example, we might say that injuries from a negligently caused automobile accident are remedied if the victim is awarded sufficient money to pay for his medical bills and compensate him for his pain and suffering.

The problem with the exclusionary rule as a remedy is that the constitutional injury stemming from an unreasonable search is not conviction for a crime that the accused in fact committed or use of reliable evidence that might prove his guilt. The purpose of the Fourth Amendment is not to prevent guilty people from being convicted. Instead, the injury the Fourth Amendment is designed to avoid is invasion of the accused's autonomy and privacy.

There is no logical, remedial connection between this injury and the suppression of evidence. If a police officer negligently runs down a pedestrian who happens to be escaping after robbing a bank, we don't say that the robber can keep the money he has stolen. The harm we care about is the physical injury caused by the accident, not the failure to get away with the robbery. It is therefore sufficient for the police officer to pay for this injury.

Similarly, if the police conduct an unreasonable search or seizure, the harm we care about is not the conviction of a guilty perpetrator, but the embarrassment, humiliation, or physical injury caused by the unconstitutional conduct. As a remedial matter, it is therefore enough to pay a victim compensation for these injuries. There is no reason to believe that the value to the defendant of suppression of evidence corresponds to the amount that compensates for the injuries we care about. If a minor invasion of Fourth Amendment rights prevents a defendant from being convicted of murder, compensation in the form of exclusion of evidence necessary for conviction is much too high. If a very serious invasion prevents no more than a defendant being put on a short period of probation, the compensation is much too low.

The modern Court has nonetheless continued to require the exclusion of some evidence, not because exclusion remedies a past violation but because it deters future violations. If a police officer knows that she will be unable to use the results of an illegal search, then she is less likely to engage in the illegality, or at least so the Court has supposed. But how much deterrence is required? It is here that the problem of constitutional disobedience emerges.

The modern Court has determined the scope of the exclusionary rule by balancing the costs of exclusion against the deterrent efficacy of the rule in various situations. For example, it has held that when a police officer relies on a search warrant signed by a judge when the warrant is apparently valid but actually unconstitutional, the cost of exclusion is high because, the Court thinks, application of the exclusionary rule to cases like this would lead to the acquittal of a relatively large number of guilty defendants. On the other hand, the deterrent efficacy is low because only a relatively small number of illegal searches will be prevented. The exclusionary rule therefore does not apply in this situation. Given the Court's political predilections, it is unsurprising that the Court has used this technique to avoid application of the rule in a large and growing number of situations.

Liberals have forcefully objected to these decisions, but, for our purposes, the most important point is that not even liberals think that the government is obligated to prevent every single Fourth Amendment violation. If there were such an obligation, the exclusionary rule would be the least of our worries. Offending police officers would have to be

sentenced to life imprisonment or perhaps even executed. No one believes that these measures are required. Anyone who thinks seriously
about it realizes that there is an optimal level of constitutional violation.
At some point, the cost of preventing additional violations simply isn't
worth it. There is no disagreement about whether the Constitution
should sometimes be violated. The only real disagreement is about how
many constitutional violations should be tolerated.

Of course, there is a sense in which we do not "want" these violations to occur any more than we "want," say, traffic deaths or murders.
In a perfect world, with no costs of prevention, we would have no traffic
deaths, no murders, and no constitutional violations. But we do not live
in a perfect world. Constitutional obedience imposes costs. If it did not,
there would never be a temptation to disobey. Our exclusionary rule
jurisprudence demonstrates that when the costs are too high, we give in
to the temptation and choose disobedience.

Much the same analysis lies behind the Court's approach to the
doctrine of stare decisis, but whereas the exclusionary rule implicates
future constitutional violations, stare decisis involves a violation in the
very case before the Court. The doctrine holds that in many cases the
Court should follow its own prior decisions. It is not an inflexible command. As we have already seen, some of the Court's most famous decisions have overruled prior decisions. Still, even a casual glance at the
Court's opinions makes clear that the doctrine is central to much of the
Court's work. In the vast majority of these opinions, the justices spend
little or no effort examining constitutional text and history. Instead, the
justices parse their own prior decisions. They do so because it is usually
these decisions, rather than the Constitution itself, that will determine
the outcome of the case.

Although it may not be immediately apparent, the doctrine of stare
decisis amounts to an elaborate justification for constitutional violation. This is so because the doctrine only takes hold when the justices
currently think that a prior decision is incorrect. After all, if the prior

decision were correct, then it should be followed not because of stare decisis but because the Constitution itself commands this result. Put differently, it is only in cases where the prior decision is incorrect that that decision itself makes a difference. At least in principle, when the prior decision is correct, the current court should reach the same result even if there had been no prior decision. Because stare decisis is a doctrine about respect for prior decisions, it follows that it applies only in cases where previous justices got it wrong. And, of course, to follow their wrong decision now is to engage in constitutional disobedience.

In some cases, a conscientious justice will be uncertain whether a particular decision is right or wrong. But notice in this regard that stare decisis is different from mere judicial modesty. A sensible judge might realize that she does not have exclusive access to the truth and might weigh the fact that prior judges have come to a particular conclusion before reaching her own judgment on a constitutional question. When a judge is not sure what the right outcome is, she might simply defer to the judgment of her predecessors.

Similarly, judges might treat prior opinions in the same way that they treat briefs, arguments made by learned commentators, or, more controversially, decisions made in other legal systems. But judges who make an all-things-considered judgment about the right outcome are not following the doctrine of stare decisis, at least as I am using the term here. The doctrine does not apply even when a judge is influenced by the arguments made in prior opinions or takes into account the wisdom of her predecessors. This is because the judgment a judge reaches when she relies on these factors is still ultimately her own. Stare decisis takes hold only after the judge has reached this personal judgment. The doctrine requires her to disregard that judgment, not because she has been persuaded by other material, but despite the fact that she has not been persuaded. Perhaps, for example, the judge thinks that even after taking into account the views of other judges, the Constitution demands overruling their prior decisions. The doctrine of stare decisis means that, at least in some cases, the judge should ignore this judgment and adhere to decisions that she believes are wrong.

The Supreme Court has developed an elaborate jurisprudence explaining when the doctrine applies and when it does not. The Court has said that it will take into account factors like reliance on past decisions, the extent to which the old rules are "workable," the extent to which prior holdings have been eroded by later ones, and how egregiously wrong the prior decisions are. As these criteria make clear, the Court is, in effect, doing exactly what it does in the exclusionary rule context. It is weighing the harm done by continued constitutional violations against the cost of correcting those violations. Sometimes, the doctrine says, the costs are too high.

Some defenders of the doctrine have responded to this argument by insisting that stare decisis is, itself, a constitutional command. They point to the fact that at the time of the framing, judges regularly followed their own precedents and argue that stare decisis is built into what the framers meant by the "judicial power." This argument has the same structure as the constitutional argument for judicial supremacy. Just as the Constitution itself might be read to give judges the last word on the meaning of constitutional text, so, too, it might be read to require judges to obey their own prior, erroneous decisions. If seeming departures from the Constitution's substantive commands are, themselves, required by the Constitution, then they should not be treated as departures at all.

If this argument sounds paradoxical, that's because it has truly radical and implausible implications. Treating stare decisis as a constitutional command effectively allows it to swallow up all of the rest of the Constitution, at least in so far as judicial enforcement is concerned. Moreover, when combined with judicial supremacy, the effect goes beyond judicial enforcement. Taken together, the two doctrines mean that all branches of government are sometimes obligated by the Constitution itself to disobey the Constitution's substantive commands even in circumstances where everyone now recognizes that those commands are being violated.

To see why this is so, imagine an extreme, limiting case. Suppose that the Supreme Court explicitly stated in an opinion that it was not bound by the Constitution at all and could do whatever it wanted. Once having said this, stare decisis, strictly adhered to, would mean that future Courts would have to treat the Constitution as a dead letter. Moreover, even though these future Courts recognized that its prior declaration was itself unconstitutional, all other branches of government would be obligated to obey it. In other words, such a decision would mean permanent victory for my campaign to stamp out constitutional obligation. Yet if stare decisis itself is really a constitutional command, this victory would be achieved on the basis of constitutional compliance. A constitution that recognizes its own meaninglessness in this fashion is hardly worth worrying about.

A fair reaction to this hypothetical is that it is too extreme to be useful. Unfortunately, the Supreme Court is not about to hold that the entire Constitution is meaningless, and if it ever did so hold, it is highly likely that future courts would use the flexibility built into stare decisis doctrine to overrule the prior decision.

But although real world applications of stare decisis are less extreme, they suffer from the same basic problem. The justices are unlikely to countermand the entire Constitution, but the doctrine gives them the power to countermand important parts of it. Is it really plausible that the Constitution itself gives judges this power permanently to undo substantive commitments that the framers thought important enough to imbed in constitutional text? The doctrine is especially troublesome because it empowers judges who are willful and arrogant at the expense of those who are modest and deferential. Judges who take big risks and therefore make big mistakes—perhaps, even deliberate mistakes—can count on those mistakes being entrenched, while judges who are willing to defer to their predecessors have relatively little effect on the law.

None of this is to say that the doctrine of stare decisis should be abandoned. It may well be that maintaining legal stability is more important than respecting our constitutional commitments. As should be apparent from what I have already written, I don't believe that constitutional commands should be treated as binding commitments in the first place. But for present purposes, the crucial point is that legal stability is in tension with constitutional commitment. That is why judges who apply stare decisis struggle to balance the need to get things right with the need to have them settled. Defenders of constitutionalism therefore have the argument exactly backwards: As the doctrine of stare decisis illustrates, it is constitutional obedience, rather than disobedience, that threatens order.

DISOBEDIENCE AND STABILITY

I hope that these examples are sufficient to demonstrate that constitutional violations are all around us if only we take the trouble to look for them. As I have tried to show, these violations are apparent even if we assume a position of agnosticism as to what the Constitution actually commands us to do. Of course, if we relax this assumption, then there may be many more violations. When he found out that his colleagues had voted to uphold one of Franklin Roosevelt's New Deal measures, Justice James McReynolds proclaimed that "[a]s for the Constitution, it does not seem too much to say that it is gone. Shame and humiliation are upon us now!" When he was Senate minority leader, future president Gerald Ford introduced a resolution of impeachment against Justice William O. Douglas because of what Ford believed to be persistent, numerous, and egregious constitutional violations. Modern liberals, including the president himself, regularly castigate the Court for violating the Constitution by exceeding its constitutional powers.

If my analysis is right, though, there is, or at least should be, what the political philosopher John Rawls called an "overlapping consensus"— that is, an agreement grounded in different underlying reasons among people who otherwise disagree—about the prevalence of constitutional violation. Rawls is perhaps the greatest modern defender of liberal, constitutional government which, he believed, was supported by such a consensus. The deep irony is that there should actually be a consensus about the prevalence of constitutional disobedience. Justice McReynolds, Minority Leader Ford, and President Obama would agree about very little else, and they would certainly disagree about important points of constitutional interpretation. Nonetheless, whatever their other differences, they should all be able to agree that, for example, the Supreme Court's overruling of prior cases, its rejection of some forms of departmentalism, and the very presence of constitutional disagreement itself mean that the Constitution is regularly violated.

It simply will not do, then, to insist that the polity will not survive widespread constitutional violation. At best, what we are left with is not this claim but a very different assertion—that our society is held together by the *myth* of constitutional compliance. On this view, sometimes associated with the political theorist Leo Strauss, what we need to prevent disaster is not constitutional governance itself, but a "noble lie" persuasive enough to convince naïve Americans that there is constitutional governance.

We should recognize this claim for what it is: an extraordinarily cynical and elitist view of the capability of the American people with little or no evidence to support it. It assumes that it is legitimate, possible, and necessary for the cognoscenti to manipulate the masses by deliberately misrepresenting the way that things really are.

Of course, the claim might nonetheless be correct. I will have more to say about it in the next chapter. For present purposes, though, the important point is that, whether correct or not, the claim in effect embraces rather than rejects my argument. The "noble lie" position is not that we should actually obey constitutional commands. It is instead that we should make an all-things-considered judgment about what will produce the best country. Advocates of the noble lie think that the best all-things-considered judgment is that deliberate manipulation of others will get us where we want to go. Perhaps they are right about this, but the claim needs to be examined and debated. That debate has nothing to do with what the Constitution means, what James Madison intended, or our political obligation to obey constitutional text. It is, in other words, precisely the debate that we will be able to have once the pernicious notion of constitutional obedience is dispelled.

CHAPTER FOUR

...

Disobedience and Freedom

THE PREVIOUS CHAPTER addressed the concern that constitutional disobedience might produce anarchy. Oddly, though, many defenders of constitutionalism who worry about chaos also have something like the opposite concern. They claim that the erosion of constitutional obedience would produce *too much* order.

There is a deep historical link between constitutionalism and the ideal of limited government. Many political theorists have thought that a constitution is all that stands between a potentially tyrannous government and the people. Without constitutional guarantees, civil liberties would exist at the sufferance of dangerous and self-interested wielders of government power. Nothing would prevent government officials from shutting newspapers, dictating religious beliefs, abolishing jury trials, and jailing political opponents.

This link between constitutionalism and civil liberties has played a special role in our own constitutional experience. On standard accounts, the newly proposed Constitution triggered widespread worry that an invigorated federal government might threaten the liberties of the people. During the ratification process, some supporters of the Constitution met this concern by promising to enact a Bill of Rights after ratification. Under the leadership of James Madison, the first Congress made good on this promise and, ever since, the Bill of Rights as enforced by the Supreme Court has produced a blossoming of freedom.

On this account, then, an attack on constitutional obedience amounts to an attack on the legal mechanisms that have served us so well for more than two centuries. It heedlessly and foolishly squanders our heritage of freedom.

The argument of the previous chapter provides one answer to these claims. As we have already seen, constitutional violation is currently a standard feature of American politics. If obedience were really an essential predicate for the protection of civil liberties, it would necessarily follow that our civil liberties would currently be at serious risk. If one thinks that Americans have unparalleled freedom to think and do what they want, then concern for civil liberties cannot be a reason to insist on constitutional obedience.

This argument from the last chapter does not serve as a complete answer, however, at least for people who have a less rosy view of the current status of civil liberties. Whereas very few people today would say that America has slid into chaos, not everyone agrees that our civil liberties are currently secure.

On the Right, there is growing concern about the supposed collapse of states' rights, which are thought to shield us from federal government meddling, about restrictive and burdensome government regulation, and about the decay of economic freedoms.

On the Left, there is horror that almost 2.5 million Americans are incarcerated—the largest per capita rate in the world. The putative abuses of the Bush administration's War on Terror are a fresh memory, and the failure of the Obama administration to reverse all of these measures is a current disappointment.

Elements of both the Left and the Right share overlapping concerns about the emergence of a National Security State under which the executive involves us in foreign adventures without a vote by Congress. That involvement, in turn, reinforces the government's tendency to snoop on its citizens, assert the right to detain people for long periods without trial, and hide its misdeeds by invoking doctrines like the state secrets privilege.

These concerns open the possibility that the very prevalence of constitutional violation that I describe in the previous chapter has produced a weakening of civil liberties. And perhaps the weakening would turn into total collapse if we created an overt culture of disobedience. This fear, in turn, stems from a deep suspicion that the American people cannot be trusted with its own freedom. Polling data shows a disturbing lack of support for basic civil liberties like freedom of speech and press, the privilege against self-incrimination, and the right to be free from unreasonable searches and seizures. Our history of protection for minorities is spotty at best, and current attitudes toward Arabs, Muslims, African Americans, Hispanics, and other minorities provide little reason to think that racism and discrimination are relics of a past age.

This chapter addresses these concerns. It builds upon an American tradition that runs counter to the view that constitutional commitments protect our freedom. Even as the framers debated and adopted a bill of rights, they also fretted that what they called mere "parchment barriers" would not truly protect liberty. They wondered how words on a sheet of paper would prevent people with power from using that power to their own advantage.

Years later, the great federal judge Learned Hand voiced the same skepticism when he wrote that "[l]iberty lies in the hearts of men and women; when it dies there, no constitution, no law, no court can save it; no constitution, no law, no court can even do much to help it. While it lies there it needs no constitution, no law, no court to save it." If Hand was right, then the last thing we need is scholars poring over the

Constitution as if it were holy scripture. The real question is not how to interpret a document, but how to keep liberty alive "in the hearts and minds of men and women." The skeptical tradition argues that blind obedience to an ancient text is unlikely to do the trick. Instead, we need to develop a culture of civil liberties—a culture that values argument and disagreement more than obedience—that, as Hand put it, "is not too sure that it is right." The best way to create such a culture is to encourage independent thought, debate, and skeptical engagement with various versions of liberty. So long as we feel duty bound to accept without question the version of the framers, we will never have the kind of authentic commitment that is our only source of real protection.

My argument for these propositions has two parts. First, as a theoretical matter, I argue that there is little reason to suppose that obedience to constitutions effectively protects freedom. Second, as an empirical matter, I attempt to show that historically, constitutional enforcement has not meaningfully contributed to American freedom and has probably done a great deal to harm it.

THE THEORETICAL ARGUMENT

As political scientist Gordon Schochet wrote in 1979, the fundamental principle uniting all theories of constitutionalism is that "governments exist only for specified ends and properly function only according to specified rules." Constitutions are documents that specify those ends and rules and establish that government actions not justified by the ends and authorized by the rules are illegitimate.

At first, it might seem that there is a natural connection between this conception of constitutionalism and civil liberties, and it is indeed true that a constitution that sets out limitations in advance and that is adequately enforced reduces the extent to which governments can engage in purely arbitrary or random acts. This truth, however, has tended to overshadow a more important point that should be, but apparently is not, obvious: The extent to which constitutions protect civil liberties turns on the content of the particular constitution we are talking about.

Constitutions do more than delineate a private sphere; they also authorize public interventions. The extent to which a given constitution protects freedom depends upon the line that it draws between public and private power. One could imagine, for example, a totalitarian constitution that requires the government to control every aspect of our private lives. Surely, obedience to this constitution would not advance the cause of freedom.

Of course, we do not now have a totalitarian constitution, but we sometimes forget that we once had a constitution that protected a totalitarian institution. The framers of the 1787 constitution were too embarrassed to actually use the word, but many provisions in the original constitution protected human slavery, which was totalitarian. For example, Article I, sec. 9 prohibited Congress from abolishing the slave trade until 1808. Article IV, sec. 2 required free states to return escaped slaves. Article I, sec. 2, cl. 3 provided permanent and built-in political protection for slave holders. It exaggerated the political power of the slave states by counting three-fifths of the slave population in determining the size of representation in the House of Representatives.

It is hard to claim that obedience to these provisions supported civil liberties. There were a few abolitionist lawyers who tried to argue that other clauses in the Constitution limited or even prohibited slavery, but few people and no judges took their arguments seriously. The renowned abolitionist William Lloyd Garrison was much closer to the truth when he called the Constitution "a covenant with death and an agreement with Hell."

Rather than undermining slavery, constitutional obedience served to entrench it. In *Dred Scott v. Sandford*, the Court held that the effort to ban slavery in the territories violated the Constitution's due process clause. In perhaps the most infamous language ever to appear in a Supreme Court opinion, Chief Justice Roger Taney wrote that

> It is difficult at this day to realize the state of public opinion in relation to [African Americans] which prevailed in the civilized and enlightened portions of the world at the time of the Declaration of Independence, and when the Constitution of the United States was framed and adopted....
>
> They had for more than a century before been regarded as beings of an inferior order, and altogether unfit to associate with the white race, either in social or political relations; and so far inferior, that they had no rights which the white man was bound to respect; and that the negro might justly and lawfully be reduced to slavery for his benefit.

Today, Chief Justice Taney's *Dred Scott* opinion is universally reviled. But modern critics have too often ignored the fact that Taney's sin may well have been his insistence on constitutional obedience. When his language is quoted today, people sometimes forget that he purported to be stating the views of the framers, rather than his own views.

Historians differ about how accurate Taney was. His narrow argument about congressional authority to prohibit slavery in the territories is at least subject to debate. Even his broader point might be subject to challenge depending on one's theory of constitutional interpretation. But on standard textual- and intent-based theories, his broad point was probably correct. Specific constitutional language entrenched slavery, and most of the framers intended to recognize and protect it. There is a sense, then, in which *Dred Scott* better reflects the actual intent of the Constitution's framers than the views of abolitionist lawyers. In any event, when slavery was eventually overthrown, it happened not because people felt bound to obey the Constitution, but because they were willing to fight a devastating war to change it.

Today, we face nothing like the sharp contradiction between the Constitution and civil liberties that existed in the pre–Civil War period. Nonetheless, it remains true that whether constitutional obedience promotes or hinders freedom depends on what, exactly, the Constitution requires and what, exactly, we mean by "freedom." The very idea of freedom is an appropriate site for contestation. Whether a given constitution—our Constitution—protects freedom depends not just on what the constitution says, but also on what we think freedom consists of in the first place.

Insistence on constitutional obedience tries to suppress this conflict, but, as I will argue below, suppression cannot provide stable grounds on which to build a culture of freedom. As Louis Brandeis wrote years ago, "The greatest menace to freedom is an inert people.... [O]rder cannot be secured merely through fear of punishment for its infraction .... It is hazardous to discourage thought, hope and imagination .... [T]he path to safety lies in the opportunity to discuss freely supposed grievances and proposed remedies."

Ironically, Brandeis wrote these words to argue for obedience to his interpretation of the free speech guarantees of the First Amendment. The same point holds, however, if we ask what sort of free speech regime we should have in the first place. What we need, in other words, is "thought, hope and imagination" about the kind of civil liberties we should have, not the "fear of punishment for...infraction" produced by blind constitutional obligation.

To make this point less abstract, we might differentiate between two traditions in western political philosophy, which I will label "classical liberalism" and "classical republicanism." (Importantly, these positions should not be confused with "liberal" and "Republican" positions as those terms are used in contemporary political debate.) Each tradition is rich, complex, and contradictory, and taken together, they certainly do not exhaust the possible positions one might take regarding political freedom. To keep things simple at the beginning, though, it is useful to limit discussion to these two views and to examine crude, stripped-down versions of each of them.

On classical liberal premises, freedom is associated with individual choice and the absence of public coercion. For classical liberals, the main threat to freedom is the state, which, if left unchecked, might overwhelm the ability of people to choose their own life course. On classical republican premises, freedom is associated with the ability of a society to govern itself collectively and democratically. Here, the main threat to freedom is "corruption," broadly understood as the co-optation of state institutions by narrow, self-interested minorities. For classical republicans, the main threat to freedom is private power.

Most constitutions, including our own, have some mix of classical liberal and classical republican elements, and classical liberals and classical republicans might agree on many other constitutional provisions. For ease of analysis, suppose we start by imagining a constitution that is either liberal or republican. Does respect for this liberal or republican constitution promote freedom? It depends on whether there is a match between the constitution and one's conception of freedom. Obedience to a republican constitution does little to protect the liberties valued by a liberal and might do much to undermine them. Mutatis mutandis, the same is true of obedience to a liberal constitution.

Consider, for example, the problem of campaign finance. In this context, a majority of the Supreme Court has interpreted first amendment free speech guarantees as being based on classical liberal premises. On this view, freedom is best achieved by allowing private individuals the right to decide for themselves whether and how much to contribute to political campaigns. Government restrictions on political expenditures threaten this freedom and are therefore presumptively unconstitutional. One might imagine, however, a different version of free speech that was republican in orientation. On this view, free speech is the right to engage in public self-government. Large, selfishly motivated campaign contributions threaten rather than promote this sort of free speech. On this view, campaign finance regulation is at least permissible and, perhaps, even constitutionally mandatory.

Assume for the moment that the Supreme Court has correctly interpreted the First Amendment. In our current political culture, there is no doubt that most people with a different conception of freedom feel an obligation to obey the Constitution, even when it produces results that they disagree with. As things stand now, classical republicans might disagree with the Court's interpretation of the Constitution, but they are unwilling to defy the Constitution itself. It is hard to see what the source of this obligation is. Certainly, it cannot be grounded in the need to protect freedom. After all, if the Court is right that the amendment embodies a liberal version of free speech, republican conceptions of freedom are retarded rather than advanced by constitutional obedience. From a republican point of view, freedom would best be guaranteed if the Constitution were disregarded.

Of course, a republican might claim that the Court has it wrong. Many serious legal scholars think that modern campaign finance jurisprudence perverts rather than enforces constitutional values. But if the classical republicans are right, then it is hard to see why classical liberals should favor constitutional obedience.

Suppose, though, that one is, say, a classical liberal and is lucky enough to live under a constitution with liberal free speech protections. Shouldn't people like this obey their constitution? Actually, the answer is "no," but to see why, we need to focus again on exactly what we mean by obedience. The important point is that true obedience cannot be contingent on substantive agreement with the command in question. I might, of course, comply with a command that I already want to follow. Indeed, it would be very odd if I did not do so. But I cannot be said to *obey* commands when I follow them only when and because I want to. Obedience involves recognizing at least the contingent possibility of doing something that, but for the command, I would not do.

If this analysis is correct, then the test of obedience for a liberal living under a liberal constitution is not whether she adheres to its liberal commands, but whether she would also adhere to commands that require republican outcomes. But why would a liberal do this? By hypothesis, obedience in these circumstances would defeat rather than advance the freedom that supposedly justifies constitutionalism in the first place. It follows, I think, that liberals living under a liberal constitution are not really *obeying* the constitution. They would like to persuade others—republicans—that *they* have a duty of obedience, but liberal "obedience," amounts to no more than a contingent willingness to follow provisions liberals already agree with. It is hard to imagine what reasons a liberal could offer to persuade republicans to accept a one-sided deal of this sort. The only argument for constitutional obligation that a liberal could honestly offer is that obedience by republicans promotes liberal values— a reason that is certain to be completely unpersuasive to republicans.

The remaining possibility is that classical liberals can trick classical republicans with arguments offered in bad faith. Liberals might *claim* that there is a general moral duty and try to persuade their republican adversaries that they, too, will abide by it, all the while secretly knowing that their own adherence to the constitution is contingent on it serving liberal ends. Perhaps this argument might even be reinforced by occasional, strategic examples of liberal "obedience" that ostensibly do not serve liberal interests, presumably in cases that are relatively inconsequential. These examples would be offered, again in bad faith, to demonstrate that liberals do believe in this general duty. In fact, though, these supposed liberal concessions are intended as and in reality are no more than window dressing. They are offered only because and to the extent that they fool republicans into buying into a system that more generally serves liberal interests.

Could such a strategy work? We cannot rule out this possibility. Still, there is reason to doubt that the strategy will be effective over long periods of time. For it to be effective, liberals will have to keep their true aims secret. Moreover, republicans will have to be systematically more gullible than liberals and unable, even after years of defeat and frustration, to figure out what is going on.

Even if the strategy does work, though, there is a further question of whether it should be utilized. I must say that I am genuinely ambivalent about the answer to this question. Suppose that it is really true that civil liberties, as I best understand them, depend on fooling people into thinking that they have a set of obligations that they do not in justice actually have. Is the deception justified? Perhaps it is, although it must also be noted that manipulating people into accepting a system that, by their own lights, they should reject, is, itself, a kind of denial of agency, respect for human dignity, and freedom. If one agrees with Brandeis that it is "hazardous to discourage thought, hope and imagination," then manipulation and intimidation provide an unlikely foundation for a lasting culture of liberty.

In any event, two things should be clear about this possibility. First, we are no longer talking about constitutional obedience as most people understand the concept. The point is not that people *actually* have an obligation to do what the Constitution commands, but that people can be fooled into thinking that they have such an obligation by other people who, themselves, actually reject the obligation.

The second point is that before we embark on a cynical and likely unsuccessful project of this sort, we had best be sure that it is really necessary to do so. In fact, though, as I will argue below, there is little reason to think that belief in constitutional obedience is either necessary to or effective for the protection of civil liberties.

Before we get to this argument, we need to complicate our story somewhat. So far, we have assumed that constitutional obedience is a zero-sum game—that, in our stylized example, it either benefits liberals at the expense of republicans or republicans at the expense of liberals. But it is possible to imagine scenarios where both sides might benefit from a given constitution.

Suppose, for example, that a constitution has both liberal and republican elements or that it has elements that liberals and republicans both favor, albeit for different reasons. Perhaps, for example, a constitution's free speech guarantees are liberal, while its conception of religious freedom is republican. Or perhaps in at least some cases, liberals and republicans can agree on the same sort of free speech guarantees. Might it then be in the interests of both sides to promote a culture of obedience? Might there not be a stable equilibrium where republicans agree to obey the liberal parts of the constitution in exchange for liberal agreement to obey the republican parts?

This constellation might well produce a stable equilibrium, especially since agreement might be cemented for both sides by risk aversion, the fear of chaos if the agreement collapses, and the transition costs of moving to a new constitution. The important point, though, is that the agreement will not be based on constitutional obligation. To be sure, there will be the *appearance* of obedience. Each side will comply with the Constitution's terms. But actions that, as a contingent matter, parallel constitutional requirements are not necessarily motivated by the obligation of obedience. The situation I have described is somewhat more complex than our original scenario, but the basic structure remains unchanged. Each side complies with the constitution's terms, but its willingness to do so extends no further than to the cases where its interests are served by compliance. Liberals are following republican rules and republicans, liberal rules not because of a genuine obligation to obey the rules, but because of a contingent judgment that this is the best way to achieve liberal and republican ends. As soon as the contingency changes, each side will stop following the rules. Yet it is precisely in those cases where obedience does not advance a particular side's interests that true obedience is tested.

To make the same point in a different way, there is nothing about having a constitution or about having a culture of constitutional obligation that promotes stable equilibria of the sort I have just described. On the contrary, the rigidity of constitutional requirements might obstruct a deal that might otherwise have been reached. Constitutional obedience limits the range of possible bargains and so prevents some arrangements that might be beneficial to all sides. If people were freed of constitutional obligation, there is every reason to suppose that they would reach a bargain that serves their interests.

Consider in this regard path-breaking work by New York University Law Professor Daryl Levinson on the reasons for constitutional obedience. Levinson is puzzled by the fact that in the United States, political actors seem to obey constitutional commands in circumstances when it appears to be in their interests to ignore them. When presidential terms end, we see presidents leave office; when powerful political figures are criticized by their opponents, we do not see the criticism followed by lengthy jail terms. Why, he asks, is there so much constitutional compliance?

Levinson suggests numerous mechanisms that push toward compliance. For example, sometimes when people do not care much about substantive outcomes, coordination may be more important than substantively right answers. It is more important to settle which side of the road people will drive on than to come to a "right" answer. Similarly, even if four years is not the optimal length for a presidential term, it is better to have the matter settled than to continue to argue about it. Even if there is serious disagreement, sometimes stable arrangements will result when different groups have to deal with each other repeatedly over time. Game theorists have demonstrated that a "tit-for-tat" strategy, where each side threatens the other with punishment if they depart from the agreement, can enforce such arrangements.

Even when this strategy fails, existing political arrangements may be reinforced by a feedback loop. The arrangements serve to empower groups which, once empowered, use their power to protect those arrangements. For example, the Constitution's free speech guarantees led to the creation of vast media enterprises that, in turn, have a vested interest in protecting free speech guarantees.

Finally, once particular arrangements are in place, people gradually become acculturated to them, make investments of various kinds contingent on their continuation, and, hence resist change.

Where Levinson goes wrong, I think, is in his claim that these factors lead to *constitutional* compliance. Although he is not as clear about the point as he might be, Levinson seems to think that these are the mechanisms that make constitutions possible. Actually, though, they are the mechanisms that make constitutions unnecessary. What Levinson has really demonstrated is that even in circumstances where people are acting in their self-interest and do not feel a moral obligation to obey a constitution, they can nonetheless generate relatively stable arrangements.

Levinson's main focus is on institutional structure, and he thinks that the mechanisms he describes will be most successful in entrenching institutions. Importantly, though, the mechanisms can also entrench civil liberties. For example, even if our current electoral system is less than ideal, and even if we were free to change it by modifying who has the franchise, many people might feel that it not worth the strife and uncertainty to rethink it from the bottom up. Similarly, so long as our political system is relatively fluid, people who have power now may worry about what will happen when they no longer have power. They may be willing to forego some exercises of power in exchange for a credible promise by the other side that it will do the same in the future. Moreover, our system of civil liberties has been around for many years. People are used to the protections it provides and have come to cherish them even when the protections give power to their opponents. Politicians have invested time and effort in learning how to use our current system to their advantage. They are therefore unlikely to favor jettisoning it for a new one, especially if they cannot be certain what the new one will look like.

These mechanisms function not because people think that they have an obligation to obey constitutional provisions, but because it is in their self-interest to act in a particular way. Indeed, the starting point for Levinson's argument is that an unenforced sense of moral obligation to obey a text—a "parchment barrier"—is unlikely to account for the restraint of political actors. The article's important contribution is to demonstrate that we can account for this restraint without positing the existence of constitutional obligation.

Of course, these self-enforcing mechanisms do not work perfectly. They might break down. But we need to qualify this point in two ways. First, it is not so clear what should count as a breakdown. The mere fact that equilibrium is upset does not mean that civil liberties have been diluted. After all, the Civil War upset a deeply entrenched, self-enforcing equilibrium, but it produced more, rather than less, freedom. And we don't want to lose sight of the point that we are often in disagreement about what should count as freedom.

The second point is that even if self-enforcing mechanisms sometimes fail, there is no reason to believe that constitutional obligation will work better. In fact, as I hope to demonstrate in the next section, our historical experience with civil liberties strongly supports the claim that constitutional obligation does little or nothing to protect freedom.

THE EMPIRICAL ARGUMENT

The previous section argues that rational actors have no reason to accept constitutional obligation. Of course, actors are not always rational. We therefore have to face the question whether it is right to fool people into acting in ways that are not in their self-interest if this is necessary to achieve our particular conception of civil liberties. My own view is that a conception of liberty that rests on manipulation and moral coercion is deeply flawed. Whether that view is right or not, though, the previous section argues that this sort of manipulation and coercion is unlikely to be effective and that, even if it were effective, it is unlikely to be necessary. "Parchment barriers" do nothing to protect liberty, but even in the absence of constitutional obligation, political actors will often develop self-enforcing mechanisms that limit government power.

The argument so far has been entirely abstract and theoretical. What has our actual experience shown us about the relationship between constitutional obligation and protections for civil liberties? In this section, I argue that there is little proof that constitutional obligation has aided the cause of freedom and much reason to think that it has actually been harmful.

In order to understand the relationship between obligation and freedom, it is necessary, once again, to emphasize an important distinction. Civil liberties might be protected simply because people with power wish to protect them. These people might, for example, want to preserve the kind of equilibrium that I have described above. Alternatively, they might think that protection of minority rights is an important element of justice, or that civil liberties prevent rebellion in the streets. Perhaps they simply have what economists call a "taste" for civil liberties. When they act for any of these reasons, constitutional obligation plays no role.

The question we need to address, then, is when, if ever, in our history people in power have made an all-things-considered judgment that it would be best to dilute or deny civil liberties but have not done so because of a felt obligation to obey the Constitution. In other words, we have to imagine cases where civil liberties not only get in the way of what an actor wants to do, but where the actor also feels no independent moral or prudential compunction to respect them. How often in these circumstances do political actors restrain themselves because of pure constitutional obligation?

Unfortunately, this is not the sort of question that can be answered definitively by any sort of direct measurement. We can get closer to an answer, though, if we make a plausible, albeit contestable, assumption about the motivations of the actors who populate different government institutions. My starting assumption is that judges are systematically more likely to act out of pure constitutional obligation than political officials. If this assumption is correct, then the frequency with which judges have enforced civil liberties against political officials provides a rough measure of the role of constitutional obligation.

The assumption requires some immediate and important qualifications. I certainly am not claiming that judges are frequently motivated to protect civil liberties because of constitutional obligation. On the contrary, my central claim is that constitutional obligation plays a minimal role in civil liberties protection. Nor am I claiming that political actors are unconcerned with civil liberties or that they are less concerned with them than judges. Again, my actual claim is close to the opposite of this position. As I will argue below, our chief safeguard against oppression derives from the willingness of political actors to respect our rights.

My claim, then, is only that judges are *more likely* than other political actors to protect civil liberties *because of constitutional obligation*. If this is true, but if it is also true that judges in fact almost never protect civil liberties because of constitutional obligation, then it follows that constitutional obligation is quite unimportant.

Why might one suppose that judges are more likely to act out of constitutional obligation? Part of the reason relates to institutional self-conceptions. Lacking democratic legitimacy, judges see their power as defined and justified by constitutional obligation in the way that legislators do not. Even proponents of "the constitution outside the courts" seem to concede as much when they claim that the overhang of judicial review discourages political actors from the serious exploration of constitutional issues that they might engage in if judicial review were abolished.

There are also structural reasons that support this intuition. Legislators, after all, are wielders of government power. Their job is to pass statutes that inject government into our lives. When a legislator considers a bill, she is required to answer two questions: Is this exercise of government power a good idea and, if it is, is it constitutionally permissible? Perhaps it is worth emphasizing again that a legislator might think that a bill is a bad idea because, for example, she believes in freedom of speech. The fact remains that the question of constitutional obligation becomes relevant only if the legislator would otherwise like to see the bill enacted. Put differently, for a political actor, government action must pass through a policy filter before the issue of constitutional obligation arises. It seems quite likely that the filter will eliminate most or all cases where a public official would need to test that obligation.

In contrast, judges have no policy filter. They must rule on the cases as they come to them without first eliminating the laws they oppose on policy grounds. The judge can either leave in place a statute the legislature has already passed or strike it down. Whereas the issue of constitutional obligation rarely if ever arises for a legislator, it is pressed in every constitutional case that comes before a judge. For that reason, it is no surprise that we regularly see judges reaching constitutional judgments that they at least claim are contrary to their policy preferences. In contrast, when constitutional issues are raised in the legislative forum, we sometimes see legislators urging their colleagues to leave the matter to the courts. We almost never see a legislator explain her vote by saying that on policy grounds she favors the legislation but nonetheless opposes it because of constitutional obligation.

If judges are more likely to act out of a pure sense of constitutional obligation than political actors, then we can measure the extent to which constitutional obedience protects civil liberties by looking at the judiciary's record in providing such protection against the opposition of political actors. Since courts are systematically more likely to act because of obedience, the frequency of such cases provides an indication of how much effect obedience has on civil liberties.

As it happens, this is a subject that has fascinated many scholars in recent years, and their conclusions are virtually unanimous. Over the course of our history, judges have only occasionally moved in a forceful way to counter the all-things-considered judgment of political actors when civil liberties were at risk.

For example, in the early years of the Republic, Congress enacted the Alien and Sedition Acts, which constituted perhaps the most egregious violation of First Amendment rights in our nation's history. The laws prohibited criticism of government officers, and Federalist officials used them to prosecute and jail large numbers of Republican politicians and newspaper editors. The Supreme Court never had occasion to rule on the constitutionality of the acts, but lower court federal judges enforced the laws with gusto.

Throughout the Progressive Era, the Supreme Court did little or nothing to counteract pervasive violations of the civil rights of African Americans. On the contrary, with only a very few exceptions, the Court upheld racially discriminatory laws. The Court finally struck down racial segregation in the mid-1950s, but only after approximately half the country had come to oppose it and, then, only with a symbolic decision that remained almost entirely unenforced. A few years after the decision, the Court, in a much publicized case, ordered the desegregation of the Little Rock, Arkansas, school district, but the Little Rock case stood pretty much alone. Serious enforcement did not come until the 1960s, when southern segregationists suffered major defeats at the polls. When white backlash emerged and the political winds shifted again, the Court quickly retreated.

During World War I, the Wilson administration used the newly enacted Espionage Acts to jail leading opponents of the war, including Eugene Debs, who secured almost a million votes for president while sitting in his jail cell. In the infamous "Palmer raids," named for Wilson's attorney general, A. Mitchell Palmer, the administration rounded up thousands of alleged anarchists and summarily jailed and deported many of them. The courts did nothing to stop the Palmer raids, and the Supreme Court upheld all the Espionage Act convictions, albeit over famous dissents by Justices Holmes and Brandeis. Eventually, those dissents became the law, but only after the war ended and the political branches were no longer interested in jailing dissenters.

During World War II, the Court upheld the forced relocation of thousands of loyal Japanese American citizens to what amounted to concentration camps solely because of their national background. It also upheld the execution of American citizens alleged to be enemy saboteurs after hasty findings by a military commission and without the benefit of formal trials.

At the tail end of the McCarthy period, the Warren Court decided a few cases that reined in the persecution of leftists and liberals, but it did not act until passions had cooled. During the height of the panic, the Court upheld the criminal conviction of the leading American Communists.

In our own time, the Supreme Court has protected some rights of gay men and lesbians, but only after a seismic change in public opinion made the cause respectable. Similarly, its wavering course on abortion rights closely tracks the preferences of the median voter. It has imposed some symbolic limits on the government's ability to hold alleged terrorists without charge, but has done little or nothing to put real teeth into the restrictions. Meanwhile, it upheld the constitutionality of a sweeping measure prohibiting material support to terrorists that would, among other things, criminalize the filing of a legal brief on behalf of a terrorist organization.

The bottom line, then, is that even though courts are more likely to act out of constitutional obligation than political officials, courts have done relatively little to protect minority rights. Of course, there are counter examples. As we have already seen, the pre–Civil War Court upheld the rights of slave holders. During the first third of the twentieth century, the Court intermittently invalidated redistributive and regulatory legislation. The Warren Court issued a series of unpopular decisions protecting criminal defendants and outlawing prayer in public schools. The modern Court has protected property rights, the right to commercial and sexually explicit speech, the rights of white people threatened by affirmative action, the right of corporations to spend money on political speech, and the right of fringe groups to picket at the funerals of dead soldiers.

In some ways, though, these are not counterexamples at all. They would be counterexamples only if these decisions reflected constitutional obedience, rather than the Court's own policy preferences. I have claimed that judges are more likely than members of the political branches to act out of constitutional obligation, but it does not follow that even judges so act very often. Judges may have been following constitutional commands as they best understood them in some or all of these cases, but even if they were, constitutional obligation is relevant only if, but for that obligation, they would have reached a different decision. There is no way to know with certainty what motivates judicial and political actors. Given the open texture of the relevant constitutional commands, though, and given the otherwise surprising overlap between these judicial decisions and the known political preferences of the justices who wrote them, one must wonder how many of the decisions deviated sharply from the all-things-considered preferences of the justices.

Indeed, the justices frequently don't even bother to distinguish between constitutional obligation and their all-things-considered preferences. For example, the modern court's decisions protecting the white "victims" of affirmative action hardly mention constitutional text or the legislative history of the text. Instead, the Court has focused on what it considers the baleful moral and practical consequences of affirmative action plans. Its opinions on the subject hardly differ from the kind of policy paper one might expect from a think tank or a presidential commission. Similarly, the Warren Court's decisions protecting criminal defendants had little to do with what the Fourth and Fifth Amendments to the Constitution actually say and virtually nothing to do with the practice at the time of the framing. They had everything to do with the Court's deep concern about the fairness of the system, especially as it related to the treatment of African American defendants.

Suppose, though, that we give the Court the benefit of the doubt and assume that its occasional efforts to protect civil liberties really do amount to examples of constitutional obedience. The ultimate question is whether we as a country are better off because of this obedience. For many people, the protection of white affirmative action "victims," of corporations that want to hawk their products or employ workers at below the minimum wage, or of property holders resisting environmental regulation don't count as an advance for civil liberties at all. Virtually no one would defend the protection of slave holders as such an advance. Do the occasional cases where the Court has stood firm against political pressure threatening rights we should care about really outweigh these egregious decisions? If not, then the case for a link between constitutional obedience and freedom has not been made out.

Of course, people with a different perspective might applaud some or all of the decisions that I have put in the negative column. These people are likely to be less moved by my argument against obedience. Still, even people who think that the Court's civil liberties record should be celebrated must confront the question of how much work constitutional obedience is actually doing. Suppose that the justices merely voted their policy preferences and paid no attention at all to the Constitution. Is it really likely that their decisions about, say, affirmative action or commercial speech would be any different?

True, if the Court were to concede that constitutional obedience had little or no role to play in its decision making, others might pay less attention to what it said. But now we are talking about the illusion of constitutional obedience, rather than about obedience itself. It is not as if we pay no price for this illusion. It means that positions and arguments get more prestige than they deserve and that people are tricked into thinking that they have no choice about matters that should be within their discretion. Open debate about whether a policy makes sense is replaced by an authoritarian assertion that there is a duty to obey. Agency and contingency are replaced by obligation and inevitability. Is this any way to advance the cause of freedom?

PROMOTING A CULTURE OF CIVIL LIBERTIES

We cannot run time backward and do a controlled experiment demonstrating where we would be if courts and politicians alike candidly focused on all-things-considered judgments instead of constitutional commands. We can take stock of where we are today, though, and compare our own culture of civil liberties with that of countries where constitutional obligation plays a lesser role.

These comparisons provide reason for concern. Polling data shows that many Americans today are ignorant of, indifferent toward, or even hostile to many of the constitutional protections for civil liberties. Defenders of constitutional obligation can cite this fact to support the view that we need obligation to preserve these liberties. But even these defenders must realize that rights will remain precarious so long as they are not valued "in the hearts of men and women."

The standard move is to compare the United States to countries like Australia and the United Kingdom, which at least until recently lacked constitutional protection for civil liberties. It is revealing that these countries seem to have at least as good a record on civil liberties as the United States, although easy comparisons across cultures are treacherous. In some ways, though, the more revealing comparison is with emerging democracies like those in the Arab world. In countries with no tradition of constitutional protection for civil liberties, constitutional obligation obviously plays no role. Yet, precisely because of this absence of prior obligation, there is vibrant debate and mass mobilization about the nature of and protection for rights. The very contingency of the rights—the very fact that they are not established and are up for grabs—leads ordinary people to value and fight for them.

There was similar debate and mobilization in our own country before there was a constitution. Years after witnessing James Otis's impassioned attack on writs of assistance in colonial America, John Adams wrote that the oration "breathed into this nation the breath of life," and that "[t]hen and there the child Independence was born." It is hard to imagine a contemporary observer making similar comments after observing a legal argument over a modern Fourth Amendment search-and-seizure motion.

Once the battles are over, there is a natural tendency to consolidate the victory by entrenching hard-won rights in constitutional text. The rights seem more secure if they are taken out of the realm of contestation and put in the realm of obligation. But this perception is an illusion resting on a contradiction. Our formal liberties may survive as a matter of habit or for the reasons that Professor Levinson identifies. But no constitution can turn them into vibrant commitments. What true civil liberties amount to is the embrace of unpredictable, uncontrollable, and unprogrammed argument, debate, and dissent—the kind of wide-open discussion that accompanied the Arab Spring or our own revolution. Obedience and obligation are the natural enemies of this sort of freedom. Our liberties will never be safe so long as they depend for their existence on the very mechanisms of repression that they are meant to combat.

CHAPTER FIVE

· · ·

Ordinary Laws and Extraordinary Arguments

IN THIS CHAPTER, I discuss two possible extensions of my argument, each of which might be thought of as a basis for objecting to it. One extension reaches downward. If, as I claim, there is no obligation to obey the Constitution, then what about the obligation to obey lesser enactments? Don't my arguments imply that there is also no obligation to obey ordinary laws? Conversely, if one thinks that there is an obligation to obey ordinary laws, doesn't that mean that there is also an obligation to obey the Constitution?

The other extension reaches upward. I have claimed that constitutional obligation is destructive of authentic deliberation because it uses an undefended premise (that we have a duty of constitutional obedience) to obstruct and divert good-faith dialogue about what actually divides us. But constitutional argument is not the only form of discourse that has this effect. People who believe in constitutionalism rarely rank the Constitution at the top of their hierarchy of beliefs. Ultimately, most people believe that something else—perhaps religious commitments or a secular conception of justice and human flourishing—

is truly basic. Indeed, part of my strategy for attacking constitutional obligation has been to exploit conflicts between constitutional commands and other fundamental commitments.

Suppose, then, that constitutional obligation disappears. Isn't it likely that constitutional argument would simply be replaced by argument grounded in these other commitments? And wouldn't resort to these commitments also serve as arbitrary argument stoppers? Constitutional obligation might be thought of as a good precisely because it is something that people with different fundamental beliefs can agree on. If the Constitution were eliminated, we would still resort to undefended foundations, but now the foundations would be profoundly controversial.

There are two possible strategies for dealing with these objections. The first concedes that each extension is justified and argues that we ought to embrace it. On this view, there is no obligation to obey ordinary law, and people should forsake other sorts of fundamental commitments that ground their arguments. As I discuss below, I think that there is something to be said for this stance. Ultimately, though, I embrace the alternative strategy and argue that neither extension is required. One can forego constitutional obligation without giving up on legal obligation more generally, and one can condemn using the Constitution as a foundation without giving up on a more general foundationalism.

ORDINARY LAWS

Consider, first, the problem of ordinary laws. Don't all the arguments that I have made against constitutional obligation in the previous chapters also apply to ordinary statutes? After all, like the Constitution, some statutes are very old and no longer reflect current values. Like the Constitution, some statutes were enacted using questionable procedures and did not fairly reflect popular opinion even on the day that they were enacted. Although statutes are not formally entrenched in the way that the Constitution is, there are often substantial real-world inertial barriers to repeal or revision. Like constitutional obligation, ordinary legal obligation requires us to give up on our all-things-considered decisions when faced with legal commands that conflict with those decisions. Like the Constitution, statutes confront us with the question of why we should ignore our best moral, political, and prudential views just because they conflict with words written on a piece of paper.

In fact, I think that there is much to say in support of what is sometimes called "philosophical anarchism"—the view that there is no general obligation to obey the law. I will not rehearse the arguments for and against that position here, except to say that the consequences of philosophical anarchism are far less dire than many think.

The fact that there is no *obligation* to obey the law does not mean that there are no *reasons* to do so. Most laws, at least in our society, at least in my opinion, are not unjust. Even when they are not required by justice, many laws serve important coordination functions. Moreover, in at least some cases, the consequences of widespread disobedience of moderately unjust laws would be worse than those produced by obedience. Perhaps most significantly, there will often be strong prudential reasons to obey the law even when there are not reasons grounded in justice for doing so. Laws come with penalties for violation, and the desire not to risk the penalty is often reason enough to obey. On all these grounds, people who reject the notion of an obligation to obey the law might nonetheless have good reason to obey. The fear that philosophical anarchism inevitably leads to actual anarchy is overblown.

I would therefore not be terribly concerned if the decay of constitutional obedience led to a more general skepticism about an obligation to obey the law. In fact, though, the issues of constitutional and more general legal obligation are separate, and even a person who is convinced that legal obligation is essential can embrace my argument that we should give up on constitutional obligation.

One reason why the Constitution differs from ordinary laws is that, at least in our culture, the Constitution has a more destructive impact on ordinary debate. Suppose, for example, that I am an opponent of a national health care statute. Without constitutional obligation, I will argue that the statute should be repealed. Issue will then be joined on the moral and policy questions posed by the statute. Suppose, though, that I say that the law is unconstitutional. In our culture, no one, or almost no one, says that the Constitution should be repealed. The argument therefore shifts from a discussion of the merits to a discussion of constitutional interpretation and doctrine—a discussion that at once raises the stakes and distracts our attention from the real issues.

Moreover, even if the arguments *against* legal and constitutional obligation were equally powerful, the arguments *for* legal obligation are stronger. To see why this is so, we need to examine more closely the various arguments that are said to support an obligation to obey the law. My strategy is to show that even if these arguments are correct, they simply do not apply to constitutional duty.

There is a vast literature on legal obligation, and I will not attempt to summarize all of it here. Instead, I will rely on a recent essay by legal philosopher A. John Simmons, which usefully groups these arguments into three categories. Simmons calls them associative theories, transactional theories, and natural duty theories. Simmons himself believes that none of these theories adequately supports a general obligation to obey the law, and I am inclined to agree. Suppose, though, that he is wrong about this. On the assumption that one or all of them require legal obedience, do any of them require constitutional obedience? I think not.

Associative theories claim that legal obedience is simply a conceptual entailment of what it means to be a citizen or, relatedly, that legal obligation is part of the network of expectations that necessarily comes with living with others under a single political authority. Even as a defense of legal obligation, the theories seem to beg the important question. The theories use definitional stipulation rather than argument to prove the existence of the obligation. They claim, for example, that legal obligation is simply built into the definition of citizenship. The weakness of the theories is that one can easily avoid the desired conclusion (that one has an obligation to obey the law) by changing the definition.

At least when applied to legal obligation, though, the theories have some superficial plausibility. It is impossible to imagine a political community without laws, so it makes some sense to say that obligation to obey those laws is built into the idea of such a community. When applied to constitutional obligation, the theories become completely implausible. If obedience to a constitution were just what it meant to be part of a political community, then there could be no political communities without constitutions. In fact, though, for several millennia, constitutions were the exception rather than the rule. Many political communities have existed and functioned perfectly adequately without constitutional obligation for the simple reason that they have functioned perfectly adequately without constitutions. And as I have argued above, our own political community has adequately functioned despite widespread and persistent constitutional violation. The theoretical claim that constitutional obligation is definitionally built into the idea of citizenship and political association is decisively refuted by history and by facts on the ground.

Transactional theories of obligation are not burdened by this unsatisfactory feature of associative theories. They rest instead on the claim that by taking advantage of a system of laws, an individual implicitly consents to be bound or at least creates an obligation to reciprocate for the benefits she derives from the willingness of others to obey. Simmons and others have powerfully refuted these arguments, but the theories nonetheless hold some intuitive appeal. No doubt, people benefit from having an organized state with a system of laws. Because such a system depends on mutual forbearance, it makes some sense to say that a person who benefits from the forbearance assumes an obligation to forbear himself.

Once again, though, whatever force transactional theories have is lost when they are applied in the constitutional sphere. Just about everyone agrees that we all benefit from a system of laws. In contrast, the central argument of this book is that we do not benefit from constitutional obligation. My claim is not that some people should get the benefit of constitutional obedience while not having to assume its burden. My claim, instead, is that all of us should give up on constitutional obligation.

A similar argument defeats natural duties theories when applied to constitutional obligation. The starting point for these theories is that having states and organized societies is an important good and that the emergence of a war of all against all that would flow from the destruction of states and organized societies would be catastrophic. From this premise follows the conclusion that we all have a natural duty to uphold states and that widespread obedience to law is necessary to uphold them.

I have already outlined reasons why we should be skeptical of the claim that the decay of legal obligation would lead to the demise of states. Even if it would, though, it does not follow that the decay of constitutional obligation would produce similar results. States cannot function without laws, but they can function without constitutions. Indeed, my argument in this book is that our own state would function much better without constitutional obligation. If the argument is correct, then natural duty theories face in the opposite direction. It turns out that all of us have a natural duty to share fairly in the arduous but important work of undermining constitutional obligation.

Where does this leave us? Suppose that many of the arguments against constitutional obligation also apply to legal obligation more generally, as I suggest at the beginning of this chapter. Even on this assumption, it does not follow that rejection of constitutional obligation entails rejection of legal obligation. Because no one in our culture argues for repeal of the Constitution, constitutional obligation distracts us from the ordinary policy debates we should be having in a way that general legal obligation does not. Moreover, as we have just seen, there are arguments in favor of legal obligation that may be dispositive. For example, if the decay of legal obligation would produce a Hobbesian nightmare, then surely that fact outweighs any of the disadvantages legal obligation imposes. But for reasons I have outlined, the (perhaps dispositive) arguments for legal obligation do not apply to constitutional obligation. Because there is nothing to outweigh the reasons for giving up on constitutional obligation, we ought to do so.

There is nonetheless a second sort of worry that proponents of legal obligation might have. Even if the abandonment of constitutional obligation does not logically entail the abandonment of legal obligation, there might still be an empirical link between the two.

The purported link derives from the fact that the Constitution serves to legitimate ordinary law. We often focus on the limits that constitutions place on government, but we tend to lose sight of the fact that they also enable governments. As things stand now, if someone asks why one should obey a federal statute, a natural answer is that one should obey because the statute was duly enacted by the means specified in the Constitution. The worry is that if it turns out that the Constitution itself need not be obeyed, this argument for statutory obedience would collapse. Put differently, without a constitution, how would we know that a measure passed by Congress *is* a law and not just meaningless ranting by a bunch of pompous and superannuated poseurs? And wouldn't doubt about what is and is not a law erode obligation to obey the law?

A full answer to these questions would require a book-length jurisprudential analysis of how one ought to define "law" as well as another book-length sociological analysis of what causes people to recognize something as law. Without undertaking that task here, though, I think we can see why we should be doubtful about these concerns.

Let's start with the jurisprudential problem. There is, indeed, a puzzle about how certain declarations gain the status of "law," but constitutions do not solve the puzzle. The problem is that for a constitution to determine whether pronouncements that purport to be laws really are, the constitution itself would have to be legitimate. But if it is really true that legitimacy must be grounded in constitutions, then a given constitution could not attain this status unless it were enacted pursuant to some preexisting constitution. And what, then, would make that preexisting constitution legitimate?

Sometimes people respond to this problem by claiming that our own Constitution gains its legitimacy from popular sovereignty. It is legitimate because it was enacted by "We the People." It should be evident, though, that this is no solution at all.

For one thing, the purported solution simply assumes that democratic legitimacy trumps other sources of legitimacy, such as those derived from substantive justice. But what is the grounding for this? Moreover, even if we assume that democratic processes are sufficient to legitimate, it is far from clear that ratification of the Constitution really did reflect popular will, even at the time of ratification. It is still less clear that it reflects contemporary popular will.

Finally, it is important to understand that there is no such thing as unmediated and free-floating popular will. Popular will must inevitably be formed and measured by certain institutional mechanisms. For the resulting constitution to be legitimate, these mechanisms must themselves be legitimate. For example, for our own Constitution, the institutional mechanisms included a national convention and individual ratifying conventions organized on a state-by-state basis. Representatives to each of these state bodies were chosen by a limited electorate and by a particular set of voting procedures. The conventions themselves utilized a particular set of rules governing debate and voting procedures. Moreover, these mechanisms operated against background distributions of political power, economic power, access to media, education, and so forth.

It is obvious that different institutional mechanisms and different background distributions might have yielded different results. The particular mechanisms and distributions existing at the time of the framing, in turn, were created by legal rules. For the Constitution to be legitimate, we would need an explanation for what legitimated these legal rules. *Their* legitimacy cannot rest on popular sovereignty because they were the mechanisms by which popular sovereignty was measured and formed.

Problems like these caused the famous legal philosopher H. L. A. Hart to conclude that there could not be law all the way to the bottom. At some point, what he called the "rule of recognition"—the rule that allows us to determine the legal status of other purported rules—must be grounded in sociological fact rather than law. As Hart argued, the ultimate rule of recognition rests on the brute fact that at least some people in society have what he called an "internal point of view" with regard to certain rules—that is, for whatever reason, they simply thought that they had a legal obligation to obey the rules. What makes our Constitution "law," therefore, is not its democratic pedigree or the fact that it was authorized by previously existing law, but the simple fact that government officials treat it as law.

If it were true as a sociological fact that felt constitutional obligation was necessary to produce an internal point of view with regard to ordinary statutes, then defenders of statutory obligation would have reason to worry about the proposals I have argued for in this book. But what reason is there to suppose that it is true? Perhaps at the beginning of our history, a constitution was necessary to establish the mechanisms of government. As we have just seen, though, the framing generation managed to produce mechanisms for ratification that they treated as legitimate and that necessarily preceded the Constitution. In any event, we are a long way from the beginning of our history now. After over two centuries, most Americans have expectations about how government works. They know, for example, that presidents serve for four years and that the Congress consists of a House and a Senate. Even without a constitution, someone who suggested that we ignore these long-standing practices would bear a very heavy burden of proof. As Hart's argument implied, as a logical matter, this knowledge of what counts as law cannot derive from the Constitution. As an empirical matter, the knowledge is simply a fact that exists in the world and is likely to remain a fact, whatever the status of the Constitution.

Some support for this argument can be derived from the experience of countries without constitutions. Laws in New Zealand, the United Kingdom, and Israel are not legitimated by written constitutions because these countries do not have written constitutions. Yet there is no evidence that these countries are plagued by ambiguity concerning the rule of recognition.

Even in the United States, not all the mechanisms of government trace their legitimacy to the federal Constitution. Consider, for example, the powers of the several states. According to standard accounts, states were not created by the Constitution. Instead, they preexisted the Constitution and served as the vehicles through which the people ceded power to their new federal government. The Constitution's Tenth Amendment preserves the power of the states not delegated to the federal government, but those powers plainly existed before they were preserved. It cannot be, then, that it is the federal Constitution that makes state law legitimate. Yet we do not see a collapse of the rule of recognition with respect to state law.

Similarly, in *United States v. Curtiss-Wright Corporation*, the Supreme Court, in an opinion by Justice Sutherland, held that the federal government's foreign affairs powers were not grounded in the Constitution. Sutherland wrote that "[t]he powers to declare and wage war, to conclude peace, to make treaties, to maintain diplomatic relations with other sovereignties, if they had never been mentioned in the Constitution, would have vested in the federal government as necessary concomitants of nationality."

If Sutherland was right, then the Constitution does not legitimate the pronouncements made by the federal government with respect to foreign affairs. Yet no one claims that these pronouncements are not law. Of course, Sutherland's analysis might have been wrong. But focusing on the soundness of his argument emphasizes the artificiality of the notion that the Constitution is necessary to legitimate law. The vast majority of Americans have never read *Curtiss-Wright* and have not spent a moment of their time pondering whether the foreign affairs power derives from the Constitution or is an inherent feature of sovereignty. Instead, people simply have a deep but thoroughly atheoretical understanding that certain pronouncements by certain officials count as law.

None of this means that without a Constitution there would be no disputes at the margin concerning what counts as law. Suppose, for example, that, perhaps because of a clerical mistake, a bill passed by the House of Representatives was slightly different from a bill passed by the Senate and signed by the president. Is the bill really a law? If people disagreed and they were not allowed to resort to the Constitution to resolve their disagreement, how could the matter be settled?

I must confess that this is a trick question. What I have described is a real case, not just a hypothetical one, and the Supreme Court had no difficulty settling the matter without resort to constitutional obligation. In *Marshall Field & Co. v. Clark*, a company resisted a levy under the Tariff Act of 1890 on the grounds that the "law," as evidenced by the enrolled bill, was not really a law because the same text had not been enacted by both Houses of Congress. The Supreme Court assumed for purposes of the case that the claim was true, but nonetheless held that the enrolled bill should be treated as law. As the Court observed:

[W]e cannot be unmindful of the consequences that must result if this court should feel obliged, in fidelity to the Constitution, to declare that an enrolled bill, on which depend public and private interests of vast magnitude, and which has been authenticated by the signatures of the presiding officers of the two houses of Congress, and by the approval of the President, and been deposited in the public archives, as an act of Congress, was not in fact passed by the House of Representatives and the Senate, and therefore did not become a law....

Better, far better, that a provision should occasionally find its way into the statute through mistake, or even fraud, than that every act...should at any and all times be liable to be put in issue and impeached.... Such a state of uncertainty in the statute laws of the land would lead to mischiefs absolutely intolerable.

In other words, the Court had no difficulty in recognizing the putative statute as a law even on the assumption that the constitutionally mandated prerequisites for enactment (passage of the same bill by both Houses of Congress) were not obeyed. It determined that the measure was a law not because of constitutional obligation, but on frankly utilitarian grounds. Precisely because doubt about what counts as law would lead to "mischiefs absolutely intolerable," the Court formulated a rule of recognition that did not depend on the Constitution. If constitutional obligation disappeared, there is no reason to doubt that a court could do the same thing.

Of course, *Marshall Field* concerned only the formal limits on law making. Suppose someone challenged a statute on substantive grounds. For example, suppose that Congress enacted a statute requiring all individuals to purchase health insurance. In the absence of constitutional obligation, no one could claim that the putative statute was not a "real" law on the ground that it exceeded Congress's commerce clause powers. Still, one could imagine someone denying the legal status of the measure without referring to the Constitution on the grounds that it inappropriately interfered with liberty or with the status of the states.

Without the Constitution to rely upon, what would a court make of these claims? Just as the *Marshall Fields* Court relied on extra-constitutional concerns to decide on the legal status of the Tariff Act, a court might rely on such concerns in deciding on the legal status of an individual health insurance mandate. Arguably, this is not very different from what courts do now when they "interpret" vaguely worded constitutional text. For example, the Court's decisions determining that there are important limits on affirmative action or that there is a right to gay sex are at best tenuously tied to the constitutional text. Rather than textual exegesis, they reflect some mix of policy judgments, interpretations of our traditions, moral determinations, and prudential conclusions. Without constitutional obligation, one could easily imagine a court deciding issues like these on similar grounds.

This is not to say that the disappearance of constitutional obligation would make no difference. The Supreme Court would no longer be able to hide behind the pretense that it was merely interpreting the Constitution. Instead, it would have to defend openly the proposition that an elite, deliberative, and reason-giving body should have a check on the political branches. There is something to be said for such a check, but of course there is also much to be said against it.

In the absence of constitutional obligation, the decision whether to have judicial review of this sort would, itself, be grounded in extra-constitutional considerations. I have no idea how the struggle over the Court's functions would ultimately be resolved, but at least the argument would be an honest one about what the Court actually does and what is actually at stake.

However the argument came out, there is no reason to think that the outcome would produce less respect for statutory law than we have now. As things stand now, people can claim the right to ignore laws because they violate the Constitution. Because the Constitution is open-textured and subject to different interpretations, our rule of recognition is ambiguous, and this ambiguity erodes the moral obligation to obey ordinary statutes. Without constitutional obligation, this reason for disregarding statutory law would no longer exist. People might nonetheless insist that enacted statutes are not "real" laws on some other grounds, but if this insistence proved too destabilizing, we could utilize the remedy that we utilize now—final resolution of the question by the Supreme Court. Alternatively, we could abolish judicial review of statutes, adopt more generally something like the "enrolled bill rule" that the Court created in *Marshall Fields*, and treat all facially valid statutes as law. Either way, there is no reason to think that respect for ordinary statutes would decline.

EXTRAORDINARY ARGUMENTS

The possibility of judicial review in this new world raises a different set of concerns, however. Courts exercising this review would presumably resort to some sort of more general principles to decide the cases before them. Perhaps the judges would begin with a presumption favoring individual liberty or, alternatively, with a presumption favoring democratic decision making. Perhaps they would resort to Kantian or utilitarian theories. Perhaps they would even refer to biblical teachings. Wouldn't use of any of these principles pose all the evils I have attributed to constitutional principles? As a functional matter, wouldn't these principles *be* constitutional?

Unfortunately, this problem would not disappear even if we chose to abolish judicial review along with constitutional obligation. As we saw in chapter 2, judicial review is not the source of constitutionalism's difficulties. Even if there were no judicial enforcement of the Constitution, other political actors might make decisions based upon constitutional principle. Similarly, in a world without either judicial review or constitutional obligation, other political actors would resort to fundamental nonconstitutional commitments. With or without judicial review, we need to ask why anyone should think that resort to these commitments is somehow better than resort to constitutional commitments.

In order to respond to this challenge, it is necessary to separate out four different theories regarding the appropriate forms of political argument. For convenience, but at the risk of considerable oversimplification, I will label them rationalist theory, existentialist theory, Rawlsian theory, and contestation theory.

The rationalist account is grounded in ideals associated with the Enlightenment. On this view, all of our opinions should be held provisionally. They are all always open to challenge, and we should abandon them as soon as we conclude that they are not supported by reason. The failure to provide a reason that one can realistically expect others to accept makes a position merely arbitrary. To insist on that position without the ability to give a reason for it disrespects the autonomy and rational capabilities of one's audience and amounts to an attempt to get one's way by brute force.

A rationalist account creates serious problems for constitutional obligation. When a constitutionalist is asked why we should forego certain actions that we would otherwise undertake, she replies "because they are unconstitutional." But for a rationalist, this response only begs the question. What reason do you have, the rationalist asks, for why the Constitution is dispositive? Of course, the constitutionalist might offer reasons, but the project of this book is to demonstrate that these reasons are unpersuasive. In any event, at least in our culture, constitutionalists are rarely or never forced to defend their stance with reasons. Instead, constitutionalists get away with treating their position as being above argument. For a rationalist, this stance is unacceptably arbitrary and authoritarian.

There is an obvious problem with rationalism, however. At some point, reason necessarily gives out. This fact makes it easy for a constitutionalist to turn the tables on a rationalist. A constitutionalist is within her rights to demand a reason from the rationalist for wishing to pursue an unconstitutional course of action. The rationalist might respond that the course of action produces the greatest good for the greatest number, or that it vindicates God's law, or that it respects the autonomy of individuals. But then the constitutionalist can demand reasons for why these commitments justify action. Just as the quest for a legitimate basis for law leads to infinite regress, so too there cannot be reasons all the way to the bottom. Hence, the worry that if constitutionalism were abandoned, the regress will necessarily end in some other undefended foundation.

A response to this difficulty, which I will label "existentialist," abandons the task of providing underlying reasons. Precisely because the demand for reasons produces an infinite regress, we should not begin down this pointless path. Any foundational reason is arbitrary and undefended. That is, after all, what it means for the reason to be foundational. We create the illusion that these reasons settle the matter before us only by failing to ask the next question down the road of infinite regress. Using foundational reasons as an excuse for action or inaction amounts to a cowardly technique for hiding our own freedom from us.

If the existentialist is right, then the entire quest for a legitimate source of political power is misguided. There are no legitimate sources; there is only power. At the base of the long chain of tedious and meaningless argumentation is human freedom and choice. All we can expect of human beings is that they honestly recognize this fact and use whatever tools they have available to lead the kind of lives they choose to lead.

Depending on one's temperament, one might find these views exhilarating, terrifying, liberating, or deeply evil. At least in some moods, just as I think that there is much to be said for giving up on legal, as well as constitutional, obligation, so too I am attracted to the abandonment of nonconstitutional as well as constitutional foundations. The entire project of trying to reason people into a corner—of imagining that there is some universal language that will or ought to definitively resolve our disagreements without the exercise of power—sometimes strikes me as naïve and misguided. Worse yet, foundational argument tends to label opponents as not just wrong, but also outside the moral universe. For this reason, we may actually show more respect for our opponents by acknowledging that our differences cannot be resolved by rational dialogue.

Still, it is asking a lot to expect people to give up on the entire project of reason-giving political discourse, and the very fact that I am writing this book demonstrates that I have not entirely given up on it. Suppose that one wants to hang on to the possibility of authentic political dialogue. Is there an argument for abandoning constitutional foundationalism even if it is replaced by a different sort of foundationalism? I think that there is. The structure of the argument I offer below is the mirror image of the argument for differentiating between constitutional and legal obligation. With regard to obligation, I argued that legal duty might achieve important *goods* not achieved by constitutional duty. Here, I argue that constitutional foundationalism creates significant *evils* not produced by other forms of foundationalism.

In order to understand the argument, we need to explore two other responses to the problem of political disagreement: Rawlsian theory and contestability theory. By Rawlsian theory, I refer to a complex of arguments, loosely associated with the work of John Rawls, that focuses on the need to advance "public reasons" for political action. Like existentialist theory, this view starts with the unsatisfactory nature of rationalism. Because reasons eventually run out, Rawlsians, like existentialists, reject the idea that political action can be justified by foundational argument. But whereas existentialists despair of the prospect of any reasoned dialogue, Rawlsians hold out the possibility of an "overlapping consensus" on nonfoundational commitments. Even if people disagree on foundations, they might have different, intersecting reasons for coming to the same conclusions about intermediate premises. For example, people coming from a wide variety of religious and secular traditions might, for different reasons, arrive at the common conclusion that human life and freedom deserve respect. Reasoned public discourse is possible so long as we restrict ourselves to arguments that derive from agreed-upon premises such as this one—that is, so long as we confine our argumentation to what Rawls called "public reason."

Rawlsian theory suggests grounds for believing that we do not need constitutional obligation. If there is an overlapping consensus on intermediate principles, that consensus might resolve political disputes without resort to the Constitution. Daryl Levinson's work, discussed in chapter 4, suggests that there might be such a consensus. If he is right, then Rawlsian theory provides another argument for giving up on constitutional obligation.

The fear, though, is that the area of overlapping consensus is just too thin to resolve some important disputes. Consider, for example, the agreed-upon norm favoring human life and autonomy as applied to the familiar problem of abortion rights. People committed to different foundational doctrines can indeed agree on principles like the right to life and the respect for human autonomy, but this overlapping consensus is too general to resolve the abortion dispute. If one tries to make the principles more specific by claiming, for example, that fetuses are or are not living humans, the consensus collapses.

Faced with this dilemma, a constitutionalist might claim that the Constitution itself is supported by an overlapping consensus and that constitutional argument therefore should count as public reasons. People in our society disagree about religious truth and about a wide variety of secular foundational doctrines, but, for different foundational reasons, they can all endorse the Constitution. Because of the unique history of the Constitution and the regard with which it is held, its commitments and procedures can hold together our political community in a way that a nonconstitutional overlapping consensus cannot.

If the Constitution is understood at the highest level of generality, this claim has some plausibility. Virtually all Americans can ascribe to what legal scholar Mark Tushnet has called the "thin Constitution"— the ideals articulated in the Constitution's preamble, in its twin promises of liberty and equality, and in the Declaration of Independence. To be sure, we are again faced with the problem that these ideals do not command a particular result in a given case. There is nonetheless much to be said for organizing political discourse around these ideals. As I have argued elsewhere, their very open texture provides a reason for why political losers as well as political winners can claim allegiance to them. The ideals therefore provide a basis on which everyone, or nearly everyone, can continue to feel an attachment to the polity. If we all strove to recognize that reasonable people committed to the same ideals could reach different results, that recognition could provide a basis for political community in a diverse society.

I find this version of constitutionalism quite attractive, but it is important to see that it has nothing to do with constitutional obligation. It is, instead, a form of constitutionalism that gives up on obligation. It builds political community precisely by claiming that we can all embrace constitutional ideals without sacrificing our political goals. A poetic constitution of this sort does not force anyone to do anything.

If we look to the Constitution instead for settlement, all the old problems arise. Why should *anyone* much less *everyone* suppose that this particular text with all its flaws and eccentricities is the best way to resolve our political disputes? As a contingent and, I hope, temporary matter, there is an overlapping consensus supporting the Constitution. In my view, however, the consensus results from some combination of three factors, none of which legitimately supports constitutional obligation. In part, it results from the fact that people now agree with the Constitution's commands. To the extent this is true, people will act in ways that parallel the commands not because of constitutional obligation, but because they agree on the merits. In part, it results from the

Constitution's open texture which, as I have argued above, permits everyone to use it for their own purposes. To the extent this is true, constitutional obligation again drops out of the picture. A constitution that allows people to do whatever they want to do does not require obedience. Finally, to the extent that the Constitution does create felt obligation—to the extent that people think it forces them to do things they would not otherwise do—it works through the kind of trickery and mystification that I have attempted to dispel in this book.

All of this leaves us where we started. If the Constitution does not lie at the foundation of political argument, and if we are not to give up on foundations, then what are the legitimate groundings for political argument? It is here that the view I have labeled contestability theory takes hold. On this view, resort to foundational principles should be permitted only when they preserve the possibility of legitimate contestation.

This approach reverses the central insight that drives Rawlsian theory. For Rawlsians, political argument should be restricted to public reasons about which there is an overlapping consensus. The problem for Rawlsians is that overlapping consensus has a tendency to either shut down or misdirect argument, at least when the consensus centers on the Constitution.

It shuts down argument because, in our culture, constitutionalists are excused from the obligation to give reasons for their constitutionalism. We treat constitutional obligation as an unchallengeable axiom rather than as one among many contestable foundational principles. A person who does not want to lose the argument must therefore redirect it. Instead of arguing whether a particular course of action makes sense, she must argue that it is in fact constitutional. This redirection is harmless and perhaps even helpful if abstract constitutional principles do no more than provide a vocabulary to express our disagreement. But when we resort to constitutional obligation—when we point to text or intent to command an outcome—the discussion that follows obfuscates rather than illuminates the issues before us. It forces us into a conversation about what James Madison and his contemporaries thought and wrote, rather than about what we should do today.

Precisely because there is not an overlapping consensus on the validity of other foundational principles, they do not have this effect. Imagine, for example, that someone claims that a legal requirement that individuals purchase health insurance is unconstitutional. Once upon a time, the great nineteenth-century abolitionist, William Lloyd Garrison, conceded that the Constitution protected slavery and claimed that it was therefore a pact with the devil. But almost no one today responds to constitutional argument by asserting that the Constitution is evil and should, itself, be disregarded. Instead, the inevitable response is that the Constitution, properly understood, clearly permits the insurance mandate. Once this answer is provided, and before we know it, we are off and running into a deeply irrelevant dispute about the meaning of eighteenth-century text and the intent of people long dead.

Now, suppose that instead of claiming that the insurance mandate is unconstitutional, someone claims that it is, say, un-Christian. This is the kind of response that Rawlsians treat as impermissible. Yet, precisely because there is not an overlapping consensus about the legitimacy of using Christian doctrine to resolve political disputes, an argument of this sort does not shut down contestation. To be sure, some people might respond to this claim by contesting the details of Christian doctrine. But many other people will respond by claiming that Christianity is an improper basis for resolving the issue. Resort to foundational doctrine on which there is no overlapping consensus therefore keeps the discussion going in a way that resort to constitutional obligation does not.

The fear, of course, is that this argument will spin out of control. Without an agreed-upon mechanism for settlement, people will resort to force and our political community will unravel. By now, though, we have already encountered this boogeyman many times, and there is no more reason to be frightened by it this time than before. As we have already seen, many societies, including on occasion our own, manage to survive and prosper without resorting to constitutions to resolve their disagreements. Precisely because we all have a stake in maintaining a political community, our disputes are likely to be resolved one way or the other. Ultimately, our willingness to reach resolution depends upon our capacity for compromise, for transcending self-interest for the benefit of the common good, and for empathic connection to our political opponents.

Common allegiance to the abstract principles of the Constitution might promote these traits. If we imagine the Constitution as a site for contestation, it might promote a sense that even people who disagree share a common framework. But this version of constitutionalism has nothing to do with obedience. The duty of obedience only takes hold when we look to the Constitution not just to frame disputes, but also to settle them. An insistence on obedience to constitutional commands as understood by one side of a political contest is deeply destructive of political community. The insistence greatly raises the stakes of political argument. Because of the Constitution's unchallenged and foundational status, a constitutional loss effectively exiles the loser from the community. Of course, people have a strong incentive to avoid a catastrophic loss of this sort. In order to avoid it, they read their own political views into the Constitution and try to exile their opponents. The result is not community, but a shouting match deeply destructive of comity and respect.

Conclusion: The Way Forward

. . .

No doubt, some readers will find the proposal I advance here utopian at best and just plain crazy at worst. Like it or not, constitutionalism is deeply embedded in our political culture and has been for generations. According to public opinion polls, the Supreme Court is by far the most popular branch of government. People on all sides of political debate regularly invoke the Constitution. To my knowledge, there is not a single mainstream public figure who has voiced even the mildest skepticism about constitutional obligation. Even in the academy, where nonmainstream views are more common and where there is widespread disagreement about the nature of constitutionalism, very few people think that we should give up on it altogether. What is the point, one might ask, of advancing a position that, even if correct, stands no chance of being adopted? Doesn't it make more sense to devote scarce political resources to projects more likely to come to fruition?

No doubt, as things stand now, there is minimal political support for constitutional skepticism. Still, I think that there are reasons for optimism. Before there can be political change, there must be a cultural shift, and virtually all cultural change seems impossible right up to the day that it actually happens. A generation ago, it was unimaginable that there would be a black president or gay marriage. Today, these phenomena are well on their way to being entirely unremarkable.

What produces cultural change of this sort? At the simplest, granular level, it is produced by ordinary individuals who challenge conventional wisdom supporting the status quo. There are easy ways to do this with regard to constitutional obligation. The next time someone makes a claim that something is unconstitutional, each of us should answer with a perfectly straightforward, but deeply subversive two-word question: "So what?" We need a national conversation that responds to this simple query, and a national conversation begins with a host of individual conversations.

Of course, I am not naïve enough to think that cultural change comes from nowhere or that it is disconnected from broad social, material, and economic forces. Individual acts of subversion must take place in a favorable ecosystem if they are to multiply and flourish. But there is reason to believe that the country is ready for the kind of conversation that I propose.

True, many Americans revere the Constitution, but this reverence cohabits uneasily with a deep skepticism produced by the obviously partisan nature of constitutional argument. It is an important fact that when media report on court decisions, they routinely identify the judges involved according to the president who appointed them. Everyone understands that confirmation hearings are political events and that the struggle over judicial appointments is an extension of ordinary political warfare by other means. No one thinks that it is mere coincidence that, say, Justice Ginsburg and Justice Alito regularly read the same document in ways that correspond to the political orientation of liberals and conservatives.

There is an obvious tension between public infatuation with the idea of the Constitution and public cynicism about the Constitution as it actually functions in ordinary political struggle. The abstract Constitution is said to be a symbol of national unity, while the actual Constitution does no more than mirror our national divisions. The situation is unstable and is ripe for exploitation by constitutional skeptics. Someone who points out that constitutional argument has become a partisan political weapon is telling people what on some level they already know. All that is left to do is to suggest the conclusions that naturally follow from this truth.

The more general perception that our political dialogue is seriously broken provides further grounds for optimism about the possibility of change. Many Americans have grown tired of harsh rhetoric that demonizes opponents and makes compromise impossible even as middle ground seems more and more out of reach. There is a hunger for a way out of this ever escalating struggle.

Even as we find ourselves more and more in disagreement with each other, we seem to have lost the tools for disagreeing agreeably. A major source of the difficulty lies in the illusion that, somehow, our disputes could be settled if only the other side would adhere to commitments that all of us should accept. In some sense, the illusion is comforting and hard to let go of, but it is also childish and deeply destructive. It is just a fact that Americans disagree about some matters all the way to the bottom, and the failure to recognize this fact entails a lack of respect for our adversaries.

Opponents of constitutionalism need to explain how the notion of constitutional obligation has contributed to this degradation in the way that we talk to each other. When arguments are put in constitutional terms, they become absolutist and exclusionary. People can have good faith and friendly disagreements about ordinary issues and can agree to disagree, but not if one's stance on an issue places one outside the bounds of our community. When zealots claim that their opponents are destroying the Constitution, they are making just this claim. They are effectively accusing their opponents of treason.

Charges of this sort have poisoned our political discourse, and a growing number of citizens understand this fact. It is a short step from this understanding to the conclusion that our disagreements ought not to be expressed in terms of constitutional obligation. With the country in crisis and with the emergence of real questions about the future of American power and prosperity, we can no longer afford pointless rhetorical battles of this sort. Even when we disagree about fundamental values, we must learn to express our disagreement in terms that do not invoke our nation's supposedly defining commitments. More generally, though, we need to stop posturing about fundamental values and begin an open and good faith discussion about what will work.

To be clear, I harbor no illusions that the Supreme Court will stop declaring laws unconstitutional in the immediate future or that the constitutional law classes I regularly teach will soon be dropped from the law school curriculum. But even if we cannot completely and immediately kick our constitutional law addiction, we can soften the force of constitutional obligation.

If we would only acknowledge what should be obvious to everyone—that constitutional language is broad enough to encompass an almost infinitely wide range of positions—we might have a very different attitude about the obligation to obey. It would then become apparent to us that people who disagree with us about the Constitution are not violating sacred text. Instead, we are all invoking a common vocabulary to express aspirations that, at the broadest level of generality, everyone can embrace. Of course, that does not mean that people agree at the ground level. If we are not to abandon constitutionalism entirely, then we might at least understand it as a site for contestation, not a source for answers. Once it is so understood, the idea of obedience takes on a wholly different meaning. Instead of a tool to force others to give up on their own moral and political judgments, constitutional obligation becomes a demand that we ourselves make a good faith effort to understand, appreciate, and tolerate positions we disagree with.

Ultimately, optimism about the struggle against constitutional obligation must rest on a faith in the desire of ordinary Americans for self-determination. Perhaps it is just the case that Americans are not capable of self-rule. Perhaps they need the illusion of constraint provided by a sacred text just as earlier generations needed the illusion of constraint provided by the supposed divine inspiration of monarchs. Perhaps the only way we can remain united is by resort to the unquestioned authority of dry words written by dead people. Perhaps the very project of rule by "We the (living) People"—paradoxically invoked in the Constitution itself—is a stupid enterprise. Perhaps all these things are true. If so, then constitutional obligation is here to stay.

My hope is that these things are not true. We cannot know for sure until we give constitutional disobedience a try. And that is reason enough to make the effort.

Acknowledgments

. . .

This book would not exist were it not for Geoffrey Stone, who generously offered me the opportunity to write it, guided me to an appropriate topic, and carefully and insightfully edited the final manuscript. Among his many talents, Geof has the rare ability to make more plausible an argument with which he deeply disagrees. I am deeply grateful for his encouragement, support, and, especially, for his friendship over the past forty years.

David McBride, my editor at Oxford University Press, read the entire manuscript and made countless improvements. As great editors do, he combined just the right mix of flattery and criticism to motivate me to make changes that greatly strengthen the book.

My wonderful research assistant, Melissa Stewart, spent countless hours tracking down sources and editing the draft. I am especially grateful to her for summoning the courage to tell me when my argument was longwinded, unintelligible, or just plain unconvincing. She was invariably right, and on at least some occasions I was able to fix the problems that she identified. I am grateful as well to Anna Selden, who meticulously proofread the final draft.

It was in no sense part of her job, but my assistant Betsy Kuhn nonetheless volunteered to read the manuscript. She provided scores of helpful comments. I am grateful, as well, to my colleagues Guyora Binder, Laura Donahue, and Martin Lederman for their help. For very different reasons, all of them disagree with my thesis (I take some solace from the fact that they can't all be right), and none of them would want to be blamed for the end product. Like it or not, they cannot get around the fact that they contributed in important ways to the project.

Although I did not ask him to do so, and although he has much better things to do with his time, my brother, Bob Seidman, read the manuscript and uncovered an important mistake. For this, and for the many other times over the course of our lives when he has saved me from serious embarrassment, I am deeply grateful.

Three old and dear friends deserve special acknowledgment. For my entire professional career, my own test for the value of my work has been whether Mark Tushnet approves of it. I almost always ask him, and, in truth, sometimes he does and sometimes he doesn't. I am close enough to him to be grateful for his candor and he is close enough to me to provide it. His commitment to honesty means that his praise is especially valuable. On this occasion, he provided support, affirmation, and encouragement at a point when I needed it most.

Gary Peller has been my colleague for almost a quarter century. We have been through many political, intellectual, and personal struggles together, and his support for me and for this project mean more than I can say.

For many years, I have intermittently cotaught a course on constitutional theory with Michael Klarman. Although I've greatly enjoyed this collaboration, working with Michael can also be quite intimidating. He is frighteningly smart, knowledgeable, and articulate—not to mention almost a foot taller than I am. Our standard format is to argue about basic issues of constitutional theory in front of the students. In recent years, though, without quite realizing that it was happening, I've found myself parroting rather than countering his arguments. Now, I've written a book that shamelessly relies on his insights and world view.

When I first thought about the topic for this book, I went to my colleague and close friend, Steve Goldberg, to talk about it. As always, he was full of good ideas and encouragement. I would love to know what he thinks of the final product, but his tragic and untimely death means that I will never find out. I think about Steve every day, and, although he is no longer with us, his professional and personal example continues to guide my life.

Nothing is possible without peace at the core, and my wife, Judy Mazo, has provided me with this gift for more than two decades. This book is for her.

Sources

...

INTRODUCTION: THE GAUDY CONTRADICTIONS
OF AMERICAN CONSTITUTIONALISM

Ackerman, Bruce, We the People: Transformations (1998)

Ackerman, Bruce & Katyal, Neal, *Our Unconventional Founding*, 62 U. Chi. L. Rev. 475 (1995)

Holton, Woody, Unruly Americans and the Origins of the Constitution (2007)

Klarman, Michael J., *Antifidelity*, 70 S. Cal. L. Rev. 381 (1997)

Klarman, Michael J., *What's So Great about Constitutionalism*, 93 Nw. L. Rev. 145 (1998)

Kramer, Larry D., The People Themselves: Popular Constitutionalism and Judicial Review (2004)

Maier, Pauline, Ratification: The People Debate the Constitution, 1787–1788 (2010)

Roosevelt, Franklin D, President of the United States, Address on Constitution Day, Washington, DC (September 19, 1937), in 1 The Public

Papers and Addresses of Franklin D. Roosevelt 359 (Rosenman, Samuel I., ed. 1941)

Rucker, Philip & Fahrenthold, David A., "After Wrangling, Constitution Is Read on House Floor, Minus Passages on Slavery," Wash. Post, January 7, 2011

Steinhauer, Jennifer, "Constitution Has Its Day (More or Less) in House," N.Y. Times, January 7, 2011, at A15

CHAPTER ONE: THE ARGUMENT BRIEFLY STATED

Breyer, Stephen G., Active Liberty: Interpreting Our Democratic Constitution (2008)

Constitutionalism: Philosophical Foundations (Alexander, Larry, ed. 2008)

Holton, Woody, Unruly Americans and the Origins of the Constitution (2007)

Levinson, Sanford, Our Undemocratic Constitution: Where the Constitution Goes Wrong (and How We the People Can Correct It) (2008)

Marbury v. Madison, 5 U.S. (1 Cranch.) 137 (1803)

Pennock, J. Roland & Chapman, John W., eds., Constitutionalism (1979)

Rehnquist, William H., The Notion of a Living Constitution, 54 Tex. L. Rev. 693 (1976)

Scalia, Antonin, Originalism: The Lesser Evil, 57 U. Cin. L. Rev. 849 (1989)

Strauss, David, The Living Constitution (2010)

CHAPTER TWO: OBEDIENCE OVER TIME

Ackerman, Bruce, We the People (1991)

Balkan, J. M., Agreements with Hell and Other Objects of Our Faith, 65 Ford. L. Rev. 1708 (1997)

Bickel, Alexander, The Least Dangerous Branch: The Supreme Court at the Bar of Politics (1962)

Blasi, Vincent, *The Pathological Perspective and the First Amendment*, 85 Colum. L. Rev. 44 (1985)

Bork, Robert, *Neutral Principles and Some First Amendment Problems*, 47 Ind. L. J. 1 (1971)

Bork, Robert, The Tempting of America (1990)

Brown v. Board of Education, 347 U.S. 483 (1954)

Cohen, Felix S., *Transcendental Nonsense and the Functional Approach*, 35 Colum. L. Rev. 809 (1935)

Cover, Robert M., Justice Accused: Antislavery and the Judicial Process (1975)

Dred Scott v. Sandford, 60 U.S. (19 How.) 393 (1857)

Dworkin, Ronald, Law's Empire (1997)

Elster, Jon, Ulysses and the Sirens: Studies in Rationality and Irrationality (1979)

Elster, John, Ulysses Unbound: Studies in Rationality, Precommitment, and Constraint (2000)

Ely, John Hart, Democracy and Distrust (1980)

Freehling, William W., The Road to Disunion (2007)

Friedman, Barry, The Will of the People: How Public Opinion Has Influenced the Supreme Court and Shaped the Meaning of the Constitution (2009)

Holmes, Oliver W. Jr., *Law in Science and Science in Law*, 12 Harv. L. Rev. 443 (1899)

Holmes, Stephen, Passions and Constraint (1995)

Klarman, Michael J., From Jim Crow to Civil Rights: The Supreme Court and the Struggle for Racial Equality (2004)

"Letter from Thomas Jefferson to James Madison" in 6 The Works of Thomas Jefferson 3 (Ford, Paul L. ed. 1904)

"Letter from Thomas Jefferson to Samuel Kercheval" (July 12, 1816), in Thomas Jefferson, Writings (1984)

Maier, Pauline, Ratification: The People Debate the Constitution, 1787–1788 (2010)

McGinnis, John O. & Rappaport, Michael B, *Originalism and the Good Constitution*, 998 Geo. L. J. 1693 (2010)

Nelson, William E. The Fourteenth Amendment: From Political Principle to Judicial Doctrine (1988)

Parfit, Derek, Reasons and Persons (1985)

Roe v. Wade, 410 U.S. 113 (1973)

Rosenberg, Gerald, The Hollow Hope: Can Courts Bring about Social Change? (1991)

Rubenfeld, Jed, Freedom and Time: A Theory of Constitutional Self-Government (2001)

Samaha, Adam, *Dead Hand Arguments and Constitutional Interpretation*, 108 Colum. L. Rev. 606 (2008)

Scalia, Antonin, A Matter of Interpretation: Federal Courts and the Law (1997)

Schelling, Thomas C., Choice and Consequence (1984)

The Supreme Court in Conference (1940–1985): the Private Discussions behind Nearly 300 Supreme Court Decisions (Dickson, Del ed. 2001)

CHAPTER THREE: THE BANALITY
OF CONSTITUTIONAL VIOLATION

Alexander, Larry & Schauer, Frederick, *On Extrajudicial Constitutional Interpretation*, 110 Harv. L. Rev. 1359

Brown v. Board of Education, 347 U.S.483 (1954)

Brown v. Plata, 131 S. Ct. 1910 (2011)

Bush v. Gore, 531 U.S. 98 (2000)

Cleveland, Sarah H., *Powers Inherent in Sovereignty: Indians, Aliens, Territories, and the Nineteenth Century Origins of Plenary Power over Foreign Affairs*, 81 Tex. L. Rev. 1 (2002)

Confirmation Hearings on the Nomination of John G. Roberts, Jr. to Be Chief Justice of the United States: Hearings before the S. Comm. On the Judiciary, 109th Cong. (2005)

Cooper, Charles J., *Stare Decisis: Precedent and Principle in Constitutional Adjudication*, 73 Corn. L. Rev. 401 (1988)

Cooper v. Aaron, 358 U.S. 1 (1958)

District of Columbia v. Heller, 554 U.S. 570 (2008)

Ex parte Merryman, 17 F. Cas. 144 (C.C.D. Md. 1861)

Ex parte Quirin, 317 U.S. 1 (1942)

Fallon, Richard H., Jr., *Marbury and the Constitutional Mind: A Bicentennial Essay on the Wages of Doctrinal Tension*, 91 Cal. L. Rev. 1 (2003)

Fallon, Richard H., Jr., *Stare Decisis and the Constitution: An Essay on Constitutional Methodology*, 76 N.Y. U. L. Rev. 570 (2001)

Farber, Daniel, Lincoln's Constitution (2003)

Gerhardt, Michael J., The Federal Impeachment Process: A Constitutional and Historical Analysis (2d ed. 2000)

Garcia v. San Antonio Metropolitan Transit Authority, 469 U.S. 528 (1985)

Johnson, Dawn E., *Functional Departmentalism and Nonjudicial Interpretation: Who Determines Constitutional Meaning?* 67 L. & Contemp. Prob. 105 (2004)

Klarman, Michael J., *Brown at 50*, 90 Va. L. Rev. 1613 (2004)

Klarman, Michael J., Brown v. Board of Education and the Civil Rights Movement (2007)

Korematsu v. United States, 323 U.S. 214 (1944)

Lawson, Gary, *The Constitutional Case against Precedent*, 17 Harv. J. L. & Pub. Poly. 23 (1994)

Lawson, Gary & Moore, Christopher D., *The Executive Power of Constitutional Interpretation*, 81 Iowa L. J. 1267 (1996)

Mapp v. Ohio, 367 U.S. 643 (1961)

Marbury v. Madison, 5 U.S. (1 Cranch.) 137 (1803)

Mayer, David N., The Constitutional Thought of Thomas Jefferson (1994)

Meese, Edwin III, *The Law of the Constitution*, 61 Tul. L. Rev. 979 (1987)

Miranda v. Arizona, 384 U.S. 436 (1966)

Mitchell, Jonathan F., *Stare Decisis and Constitutional Text*, 110 Mich. L. Rev. 1 (2011)

Monaghan, Henry Paul, *Stare Decisis and Constitutional Adjudication*, 88 Colum. L. Rev. 723 (1988)

National League of Cities v. Usery, 426 U.S. 833 (1976)

New York v. United States, 505 U.S. 144 (1992)

O'Donnell, Pierce, In Time of War (2005)

Paulsen, Michael Stokes, *The Intrinsically Corrupting Influence of Precedent*, 22 Const. Comm. 289 (2005)

Paulsen, Michael Stokes, *The Most Dangerous Branch: Executive Power To Say What the Law Is*, 83 Geo. L. J. 217 (1994)

Payne v. Tennessee, 501 U.S. 808 (1991)

Planned Parenthood of Southeast Pennsylvania v. Casey, 505 U.S. 833 (1992)

Plessy v. Ferguson, 163 U.S. 537 (1896)

Prakash, Saikrishna & Yoo, John, *Against Judicial Supremacy*, 103 Mich. L. Rev. 1539 (2005)

Rawls, John, Political Liberalism (1993)

Reno v. Condon, 528 U.S. 141 (2000)

Riddick, Floyd M., The Classification of United States Senators, S. Doc. No. 89–103 (2d Sess. 1966)

Roe v. Wade, 410 U.S. 113 (1973)

Romer v. Evans, 517 U.S. 620 (1996)

Roper v. Simmons, 543 U.S. 551 (2005)

Shesol, Jeff, Supreme Power: Franklin Roosevelt vs. the Supreme Court (2010)

Swindler, William F., Court and Constitution in the Twentieth Century: The New Legality, 1932–1968 (1970)

The Supreme Court in Conference (1940–1985): The Private Discussions behind Nearly 300 Supreme Court Decisions (Dickson, Del ed. 2007)

Scalia, Antonin, *Originalism: The Lesser Evil*, 57 U. Cin. L. Rev. 849 (1989)

Terminiello v. Chicago, 337 U.S. 37 (1949)

Tushnet, Mark, Taking the Constitution Away from the Courts (1999)

United States v. Leon, 468 U.S. 897 (1984)

Vieth v. Jubelirer, 541 U.S. 267 (2004)

Walker v. City of Birmingham, 388 U.S. 307 (1967)

Wingfield, Kyle, "Alabama Chief Justice Removed from Office," 11/13/03, http://www.al.com/special report/?111303moore.htm.

Youngstown Sheet & Tube Co. v. Sawyer, 343 U.S. 579 (1952)

CHAPTER FOUR: DISOBEDIENCE AND FREEDOM

American Revolution Center, The, The American Revolution: Who Cares? (2009)

Axelrod, Robert M., The Evolution of Cooperation (2006)

Citizens United v. Federal Election Commission, 130 S. Ct. 876 (2010)

Cover, Robert M., Justice Accused: Anti-slavery and the Judicial Process (1975)

Dred Scott v. Sandford, 60 U.S. (19 How.) 393 (1857)

Fallon, Richard H., *The Core of an Uneasy Case for Judicial Review*, 121 Harv. L. Rev. 1693 (2008)

Fehrenbacher, Don E., The Dred Scott Case, Its Significance in American Law and Politics (1978)

Graber, Mark A., Dred Scott and the Problem of Constitutional Evil (2006)

Garrison, William Lloyd, "The Constitution: A Covenant with Death and an Agreement with Hell," The Liberator, vol. 12, as cited in Barnett, Randy E., *Whence Comes Section One? The Abolitionist Origins of the Fourteenth Amendment*, 3 J. L. An. 165 (2011)

Hand, Learned, The Spirit of Liberty (Pillard, Irving ed. 1960)

Klarman, Michael, From Jim Crow to Civil Rights: The Supreme Court and the Struggle for Racial Equality (2004)

Klarman, Michael, *Rethinking the Civil Rights and Civil Liberties Revolutions*, 82 Va. L. Rev. 1 (1996)

Lasson, Nelson, The History and Development of the Fourth Amendment to the Constitution (Levy, Leonard ed. 1970)

Levinson, Daryl, *Parchment and Politics: The Positive Puzzle of Constitutional Commitment*, 124 Harv. L. Rev. 657 (2011)

"Poll Finds only 33% Can Identify Bill of Rights," N.Y. Times, December 15, 1991, http://www.nytimes.com/1991/12/15/us/poll-finds-only-33-cab-identify-bill-of-rights.html

Rosenberg, Gerald N., The Hollow Hope: Can Courts Bring about Social Change? (1991)

Schochet, Gordon J., Introduction: Constitutionalism, Liberalism, and the Study of Politics in Constitutionalism (Pennock, J. Roland & Chapman, John H. eds. 1979)

Stone, Geoffrey R., Perilous Times: Free Speech in Wartime from the Sedition Act of 1789 to the War on Terror (2004)

The Federalist No. 48 (James Madison), http://thomas.loc.gov/home/histdox/fedpapers.html

Tushnet, Mark, Taking the Constitution away from the Courts (1999)

"'We the people'...Don't Know the Constitution, according to New Survey," ABA Journal, May 1, 1987, at 20

Whitney v. California, 274 U.S. 357 (1927)

CHAPTER FIVE: ORDINARY LAWS
AND EXTRAORDINARY ARGUMENTS

Grutter v. Bollinger, 539 U.S. 306 (2003)

Guttman, Amy & Thompson, Dennis, Democracy and Disagreement (1996)

Hart, H. L. A., The Concept of Law (1994)

Kennedy, Duncan, *American Constitutionalism as Civil Religion: Notes of an Atheist*, 19 Nova L. Rev. 909 (1995)

SOURCES

Lawrence v. Texas, 539 U.S. 558 (2003)

Marshall Field & Co v. Clark, 143 U.S. 649 (1892)

Rawls, John, Political Liberalism (1993)

Tushnet, Mark, Taking the Constitution Away from the Courts (1999)

Wellman, Christopher Heath & Simmons, A. John, Is There a Duty to Obey the Law? (2005)

United States v. Curtiss-Wright Corporation, 299 U.S. 304 (1936)

CONCLUSION: THE WAY FORWARD

Saad, Lydia, "Supreme Court Starts Term with 51% Approval: High Court's Approval Rating Down from 2009, but Exceeds that of Other Two Branches," Gallup Politics, 10/6/2010, http://www.gallup.com/poll/143414/supreme-court-starts-term-approval.aspx

Index

...